THE MOBBS' OWN

The 7th Battalion, The Northamptonshire Regiment.

by

David Woodall

THE MOBBS' OWN

The 7th Battalion, The Northamptonshire Regiment.

by

David Woodall

Published by Roger Frisby, Spratton, Northamptonshire,
in association with David Woodall.

THE MOBBS' OWN

The 7th Battalion, The Northamptonshire Regiment.
by
David Woodall.

Published by Roger Frisby. Rose Cottage, Haynes Lane, Spratton, Northamptonshire,
in association with David Woodall.

Copyright © David Woodall. 1994

David Woodall asserts the moral right to be identified as the author of this work.

ISBN 0 9524475 0 9

Printed by Axxent Ltd,
99-101, St Leonards Road, Windsor, Berkshire, SL4 3BZ

Author's notes.

It has been long suggested that there should be a book written about Edgar Mobbs as a soldier. I consider this to be important, for the Mobbs' memorial is dedicated to his memory as a soldier and the Mobbs' Memorial Match at the Saints Rugby Club which is held annually, amplifies his standing as a sportsman.

As Edgar's military career was devoted to service in the 7th Service Battalion of the Northamtonshire Regiment, then it follows that this book must also be a history of that battalion, it is impossible to divorce one from the other.

I have mentioned many names and this has been done for a sound reason. A battalion is comprised of many men and these men should not be ignored and they have their rightful place in the annals of military history.

Acknowledgements.

I must thank Joseph Sharpe who kindly assisted in the editing of my manuscript and made helpful suggestions. The responsibility for accuracy and comment is mine alone.

I am particularly grateful to Sir Nigel Seely for his consent to use photographs originally contained in a book by Captain Guy Paget published in 1915. I would also like to thank Roger Horwood, the secretary of the Northampton Rugby Football Club for his loan of the photograph of Edgar Mobbs and the facilities offered by him, and John Butcher of Irchester for his loan of photographs and original letters. Again I must thank Joseph Sharpe for making the reproductions of the photographs to which I have just referred. The Northampton Mercury Company, gave their kind permission for me to use quotations, full articles and letters, from the local newspaper between 1914 and 1922. The Regimental Museum of the Northamptonshire Regiment gave me permission to copy the war diaries of the 7th battalion and I thank the then curator, Major Baxter.

To the many veterans of the 7th, now mostly passed away. I give my thanks for their interest and patience in answering my many questions, put to them many years ago, when the nucleus of this book was an academic essay.

David Woodall.
July 1994.

Foreword.

In August 1914, it all happened. The talking and the conjecture had stopped, the war had commenced. The reality of the situation did not introduce deep concern or even trepidation. Throughout the nation a new spirit arose, it could be labelled as patriotism, or at its worst, jingoism. All were enraptured by this new vision, the vision of a quick victory over the dreaded Hun. 'It would all be over by Christmas' was a catch phrase synonymous with this time.

The next serious question that had to be asked was a simple one. Was the nation ready? Great Britain had the largest navy in the world, well trained and equipped. From a strategic point of view this was excellent because maintaining the sea lanes was vital for the nation. This was only one part of the equation, the other was a land force. The regular Army's main duty was to safeguard the outposts of the Empire and was not designed to fight a war on the continent of Europe. This small army with its headquarters at Aldershot was named the British Expeditionary Force and was the only army that the nation possessed.

From its headquarters orders were given for the regular battalions to muster and embark for France. Because of the geographical position of the Empire this only applied to the home units. The infantry divisions were made up from the County Regiments, which as a rule could supply the 1st and 2nd battalions of their regiments. This applied to the Northamptonshire Regiment and these fine, well trained and highly motivated troops embarked for France.

To see these men marching to the railway stations filled the local population with pride and they treated their troops as heroes. Alas, this had not always been the case. A regular soldier prior to this time of patriotic fervour was not sociably acceptable. A young lady seen walking out with a soldier would quickly lose her treasured reputation. Young ladies would cross the road to avoid soldiers that were harmlessly approaching them on the pavement.

Life for the regular soldier was hard. They were subjected to the severest discipline, and hours of boredom mainly due to the fact there were never enough people to fight. Dry firing on the range was common, the term 'dry' meaning they did not use ammunition because the nation would not allow them the expense and waste.

As in society as a whole at that time, there was a wide social division in the regiments. Most of the officers could not live on their pay and enjoyed private incomes. The wealth of a regiment often decided how costly an officers' mess bill would be, the wealthier the colonel, the higher the mess bill. Entertainment was often lavish and the officers had to pay for it. Fortunately for the Northamptonshires, they were not a wealthy regiment, and officers could survive without large private incomes. These officers came mainly from the local landed gentry and the upper middle classes. All officers had to supply a mount, even though they were foot soldiers. The entire system for officers was like a club for gentlemen, where fine uniforms could be worn, comfortable messes enjoyed and one did not have to become too concerned with being a professional.

With the departure of the BEF, being the nations only standing army, some considerable concern was shown by the War Office. The Minister Of War at the time was the Empire's finest soldier, Lord Kitchener. Unlike the majority of his kind, Kitchener considered that the war would last for some considerable time, resulting in heavy losses and a New Army must be recruited and trained.

Apart from the early press gangs who obtained seamen to serve in British manowars, Britain prided itself on the tradition of the volunteer, both the Royal Navy and the Army were solely composed of men who had offered their service.

THE MOBBS' OWN

This was not the case with the continental countries who had large standing armies and a vast array of reservists accrued from the system of compulsory military service.

The advent of the war very quickly proved that considerable sized armies could be easily decimated in a relatively short time, and with it the experience of seasoned regulars, both officers and men.

The BEF supplied eight divisions, followed by that of a Guard's division, as both the Germans and the Russians were operating these elite units. To assist in providing regular units for the Western Front, Territorial regiments were called to the colours and took the place of regulars in India and other outposts of the Empire. Because of this input of part time soldiers, all attached to their parent regiments and wearing the same cap badge, the BEF was supported by a further three divisions. The 1/4th Battalion, the Northamptonshire Regiment was a typical Territorial battalion, which served in Mesopotamia, and having as its adjutant, one John Brown, who later become General Sir John Brown, the first Territorial officer to reach such rank.

By December 1914, the month in which the war, according to popular opinion, should end, the BEF with an original strength of 200,000 had lost 80,000 killed and wounded. Many units were of skeleton strength and had great difficulty in holding the line south of Ypres.

The only replacements available to Lord Kitchener were the Territorial units that had been left for home defence. Lord Kitchener did not like the Territorials. It had been said that he witnessed the French reserves going to the front during the Franco Prussian war and was dismayed by their poor turnout and lack of training. Further more, unlike the regular Army, the Territorials were administered by their own associations, and Kitchener feared civilian interference and nepotism in connection with promotions. He was willing to allow the Territorials to intensify their training and be given more modern equipment, if and when available, in readiness to go to France, but that was all.

The next Army to be formed in the nation was going to be Kitchener's. It was not to be associated with the Territorials, but would become a new regular Army. Unlike the actual professional Army, men would not be asked to sign on for service of either life or at the very least twelve years service, they would be asked to sign on for the duration of the war and because of this would become regular soldiers and not suffer the reputation of being part time or weekend soldiers. This was largely influenced by the failure of the Union army in the American civil war, who lost thousands of men in the midst of a bloody combat because their two years service had expired.

The Territorial force, comprised of fourteen divisions of infantry and fourteen brigades of yeomanry cavalry, had by November 1914 sufficient training to embark to France, and Lord Kitchener immediately took steps to promote a gigantic recruiting campaign for his New Army.

To launch this New Army, recruiting committees were formed who were responsible for the advertising campaign which could only be described as social pressure. The Country needed thousands of men to volunteer, there would be no compulsory service. These new battalions would be associated with their county regiments and would be called service battalions. The country was divided into command areas, which were planned to produce six divisions.

This campaign for the first New Army appealed for single men from all classes, to enlist as patriots and fight the common enemy. By the end of August 1914 this was achieved and 100,000 men had enlisted.

After this initial thrust to obtain a volunteer army, the recruiting became fragmented and unbalanced, some areas having a higher response than others. There were numerous reasons why men should follow the call to the colours. One was simple patriotism, they felt it as their duty. Others being unemployed considered that it was an escape from the poverty of the dole. Many young men hurried to join thinking

THE MOBBS' OWN

that it would all be over before they could be trained and they would have missed out.

Kitchener not satisfied with the 100,000 men he had already obtained, appealed yet again, this time for a second New Army. By this time the papers were full of the land battles taking place on the continent and to the man in the street the matter of the war was not one that could be simply left to the regulars and the young volunteers, there was a need for all men of military age to become involved.

This second New Army was forced to make revisions, out went the stipulation that volunteers would have to be single, and men up to thirty five years of age would be considered. The response was so great that the recruiting system was stretched and came close to collapse dealing with the volume of men who desired to become soldiers.

Due to the heavy losses on the Western Front, it was realised that a vast New Army would be required and constant training undertaken, so that battalions could be replaced with trained, or at least, partially trained men.

In September, Lord Kitchener, having found that thousands of men who had volunteered had been rejected through health reasons, made an effort to tighten entry qualifications, for what could be called his third army. He tightened height standards together with standards of health, not allowing doctors to quickly pass through recruits and claim their bonus.

By this time conditions in the New Army camps had filtered through to the population. Furthermore, allowances for the mens' families had been bogged down by the size of the problem and many families were close to starvation. The War Office could not contend with these payments and it was not until allowances could be paid through post offices that the problem could be dealt with. This alone had a detrimental effect upon recruiting married men, who were reluctant to leave their families to the mercy of the state.

11

The losses at the front had to be replaced. It was realised by Parliament that the war was going to swallow vast amounts of men. The French army was being bled to death, having over 350,000 casualties in the first few months of the war. Great Britain had to take her part on the continent and from a purely logistical point of view suffer her share of casualties.

The Parliamentary Recruiting Committee, which was arranged from a cross section of political parties, was compelled to make the nation aware of the need for recruits. Local committees had to arrange meetings and two million posters were printed and hoarded together with twenty million leaflets. The recruiting campaign was little different from that of an election campaign, local agents were appointed and house to house canvassing took place. The system still failed to bring forth the required amount of men.

Within the nation the influences of the war were felt. Many industries came to a sudden standstill, shedding their labour forces, who in turn became ideal recruits for the Army. Men going to the labour exchange for either assistance or job vacancies, were openly encouraged to enlist. Some companies, feeling that the war would not last long, encouraged their men to enlist, promising them that their wages would be made up in their absence and their places kept open for them. Members of the landed gentry insisted that a percentage of their male servants should join the colours. It was a time of great social turmoil, pressure was placed upon young men of military age and young ladies gave such shirkers, as they were commonly referred to, a white feather.

Social and economic factors, throw backs from the Victorian and Edwardian age still plagued the New Army. It was found that many men under training, found the physical demands made upon them too much, they were not fit. Years of squalid housing and generations suffering from malnutrition did not produce potential military heroes. A great deal of this problem was caused by doctors being paid

THE MOBBS' OWN

2s 6d for every man they passed as fit. Honest and dedicated doctors found that they could not cope with the amount of men they were expected to examine.

During the year 1914, 115 service battalions were raised and in time during the progress of the war most of the county regiments had 10 service battalions. During peace time these regiments with their two battalions would have about 1,300 men, during the war this was extended to over 7,000. Because of the constant heavy losses it became a great strain for the nation to bring forth suitable recruits.

To improve the situation, as early as 1914, Lord Roberts who was a surviving hero from the Boer war, announced that the Army would welcome friends who were willing to join together and be posted to the same unit. The press quickly labelled this new form of recruiting as Pals' Battalions. This in itself was bound to do well. Instead of a man volunteering and finding himself posted with strangers, he could do his training with the men he knew. This concept widened, stockbrokers formed their own battalion, public schoolboys joined together forming their own battalion, and reintroducing the term 'Gentlemen Privates.' This concerned Lord Kitchener as he considered these educated gentlemen would be of better service to the Army by becoming officers. This did not deter young men from forming their own professional units and entire teams of footballers and Rugby players made their way to the recruiting centres, clinging to the promise that they would be able to serve together.

Each area of the Country produced its own type of battalion. Many were a mixture of working class men and gentlemen, others retained their identity by their trade or profession.

Northampton, was an isolated community. There was not even a direct line to London, passengers were compelled to change at Blisworth to join the main lines. The boot and shoe trade was the main industry, there were no heavy industrial companies and this happened by the fact that there was no

THE MOBBS' OWN

coal in Northamptonshire, hence the industrial revolution had passed the town. What the county did have was plenty of oak trees which could be used in tanning and healthy herds of cattle that would supply the hides. This was how the industry was born and this gave the community wealth and work opportunity.

The recruiting committee in Northampton was given a target to recruit thousands of men and this was not easy mainly due to the sudden change of the commercial climate. The war time recession, which had effected the heavy industrial area, did not affect Northampton. There was a demand for hundreds of thousands of boots and most of the local suppliers were at full stretch using all their available manpower. This was not an ideal climate to recruit men for the Army. Men who were now experiencing full time working against previous short time and even being laid off, were reluctant to allow this opportunity of good times to pass them.

What the recruiting committee needed in Northampton was a hero, a figure that could not be ignored and a natural leader of men, with a reputation that was beyond reproach and such a man came forward, Edgar Mobbs.

Edgar Mobbs had already been rejected by the Army, and this was difficult for him to accept. There had been an advertisement in the 'Times,' requesting that young gentlemen should apply for commissions. Edgar was now thirty three years of age and no doubt in the twilight of his playing career with the Saints Rugby side, he was also, a proud holder of seven international caps. The opportunity for him to commence a second career as a soldier was attractive to his light hearted and adventurous spirit, no doubt feeling that one route to fame was fading whereas another could be adopted. They rejected him because he was too old in fact one year too old!

The creation of the Kitchener Army followed by the idea of the Pals' battalions appealed to Edgar Mobbs and the

THE MOBBS' OWN

recruiting committee who quickly used him as their own local star, a man of huge dimension, a giant who was loved by all. Edgar Mobbs was the one man who could instil patriotic fervour into the men of Northamptonshire.

The following story, is the story of Edgar Mobbs and his 7th battalion the Northamptonshire Regiment. Older readers might remember the man, others will have heard of him and some will have wondered why there is a Mobb's Memorial Match every year at the Saints. Why is there a statue of Edgar Mobbs in the Garden Of Rest in Abington Square, who was this man?

During the Great World War 1914/18 the Northamptonshire Regiment had many battalions. As already noted the regular battalions were the 1st and the 2nd. The 1/4th battalion under John Brown was a territorial battalion comprised of men who were much maligned by Lord Kitchener in the early days of the war. This battalion gained its fame by fighting the Turks. The 6th Service Battalion claimed itself a reputation in France in 1914 under the command of Colonel Ripley who was fatally wounded. These battalions were on active service before the 7th battalion was trained and equipped. Once the 7th came onto the scene they were the darlings of the local press. The men who joined Edgar Mobbs, who entered the Army as a private, were eventually formed into 'D' Company of the 7th Battalion and they became the elite of the Northamptonshire recruiting campaign.

15

One

Edgar Mobbs was born on the 29th June 1882, and was the third son of his parents. Entering the family business after being educated at Bedford Modern School, he eventually became a director of the Pytchley Autocar Company and when the war commenced he was in charge of the company's Market Harborough Branch.

The Mobbs' family lived in Onley, but it was in Northampton where Edgar gained his international fame. It has been quoted that he was the greatest footballer the town has produced. By accepting this quote it must be remembered that it was made in 1914. His sporting career can only be classed as outstanding and it would be difficult to match any other player from the club's history.

In his early school days, Edgar, displayed little prowess as an athlete apart from being a reasonable tennis player. There may have been good reasons for this. Young Mobbs was a bus boy, leaving his school every day and catching the bus to return to his family home at Onley. Young men who were boarders at the school held a distinct advantage over the bus boys, as they could be coached after school had finished. As is partially true today, the public school system evoked a strong sense of tradition in a boy's prowess on the playing field and any young man of ambition would work hard to gain school colours. In many cases this was just as important as academic success. Edgar only managed to gain a place in the school's second XV and left without gaining any school colours. This may have been a reflection of character at an early age, as he did not fit in with the close, monastic discipline of a public school.

Football had no great interest for Edgar once he had left school and started his commercial life. He did manage to watch games as a spectator, but made no effort to play. To understand the importance of sport, it must be remembered that all young gentleman engaged themselves in this pursuit, whether it was Rugby football, soccer, tennis, cricket or pure athletics. The entire social scene was centred on sport, mainly due to the fact that it was mostly set outside and had a strong social connection. Of course,in these early years of the century, there were no radios or televisions, or even cinemas, to influence young people during their leisure time.

In time, Edgar,found that hockey interested him and soon became a proficient centre forward in a team which included H.C.Boycott who later gained international honours, together with J.F.Stops. Both of these men later served as officers in the Coldstream Guards. Whether Edgar tired of hockey, or simply wished to return to his old school game, he joined the Rugby club at Onley and played for them until 1905 when he joined the Northampton Rugby club The Saints. He was by then greatly influenced by Claude Palmer, who at that time was captain of the Saints and there is no doubt that Palmer persuaded Edgar to wear the Northampton colours. It was soon recognised that Edgar's proper position was in the threequarter line and from then on this was his.

For a man standing over six feet tall, Edgar Mobbs was extremely fast and he had a very strong, burly physique. His turn of speed was excellent taken with big raking strides, possessing indominatable courage, he quickly became a star, both in attack and defence.

Because of his friendly and outgoing nature, Edgar was admired by both players and fans, and in his second season with the Saints he became their vice captain. For the 1907-8 season the club appointed him as their captain. He led the Saints for a further six seasons, and would have continued in that position if his business interests had not demanded more of his time and he was compelled to relinquish the captaincy.

THE MOBBS' OWN

Many international honours came to Edgar Mobbs during his sporting career. In 1908-9 he played for England against Australia. This match took place at Blackheath and Edgar as expected, played a great game, only to find that he was dropped from the English team that was due to meet Wales. One of the regular English threequarters fell out due to injuries and he was invited to take his place and he retained his place for the rest of the international games, taking part in the games against France at Leicester, Ireland at Dublin and Scotland at Richmond. In the season 1909-10, Edgar played two internationals, playing against Ireland at Twickenham, and leading the English side to victory over the French in Paris.

The term: A Leader Of Men, is perhaps, a hackneyed phrase, often over used and having an illdefined meaning. This was not the case with Edgar Mobbs. There is no doubt that he had a friendly and warm personality that compelled men to follow him and not to disappoint him, this was true in both sport and war. Prior to gaining his first international cap, he had captained a combined side representing the East Midlands and the Midland Counties. With his inspired leadership this side beat the Australians at Leicester, the more remarkable as this was the only game the Australians lost during that season. From 1906 which was the year of his first county match, he was appointed captain of the East Midlands and played 35 games. Further leadership honours came his way when he was appointed captain of the side representing London and the Midlands against the West at Richmond, the South against the North at Twickenham and in his last full season he captained the mighty Barbarians.

Edgar Mobbs' sporting record can only be described as outstanding. Three times he scored six tries in a match , twice against the Eastern Counties , and once against Surrey. The one record he held dear, was the six tries he scored for the Saints against Birkenhead Park. Edgar's reputation was not confined to these shores. With the English side he visited

France many times, and soon became the idol of the followers of Stade Toulousian, who at that time were the French champions.

For his services to the game and on his retirement, there was a public testimonial to Edgar Mobbs. No less than fourteen hundred of his admirers subscribed and the Northampton Town Hall was packed for the presentation of a solid silver salver, a silver tankard and four silver beakers. A volume was also presented containing the names of the subscribers.

So the time had come for Edgar Mobbs to leave the sporting scene and devote his time and his talents to his commercial interests. This was not to be. The commencement of the war quickly changed events, and Edgar like all the males in the country was influenced by the great events of that time.

It would have been easy for a man like Edgar Mobbs who was now approaching middle age to rest on his laurels and devote himself to the family business. It is true that he was an early volunteer, only to find that the nation that had honoured him with international caps had rejected him. There were good military reasons for this at the early stage of the war, when the regular Army had still a major influence. On being accepted for a commission one is awarded a single star (oranges have pips). This is a probationary rank of a second lieutenant, which can be removed without the process of a court martial, where the accused can be cashiered. Once the holder is promoted to a full lieutenant, then that rank becomes substantive and can only be removed by a court martial.

In the infantry a newly commissioned second lieutenant is placed in command of an infantry platoon. As a general rule this young officer would have only just passed his teens and each platoon had an experienced sergeant, who, by tradition, cares for his young officer as well as the men. This tradition largely applies to this very day. It can be readily seen that men of Edgar Mobbs' age would not fit into this system, even though they were willing to accept candidates up to the age of

THE MOBBS' OWN

thirty two. There are no records to show just how many men of this age were accepted for commissions, it is possible that such late entries would apply to men with specialist knowledge.

Lord Kitchener then introduced Lord Robert's Pal's concept and increased the age limit. This appealed to Edgar, it was offering him the chance to join the Army and to enable him to reapply. There was no question of him applying for a commission again, he was willing to enter the Army as a private soldier.

It is a strange phenomenon, war pulls men from their civilian lives and throws them into a military world, far removed from the relative comfort of their own homes. For however poor men might be, the majority of them had their own front doors. The cliche that 'An Englishmans' Home Is His Castle', is very apt in attempting to understand this call to the colours. Edgar could have had no military ambitions, there is no record of him having served as a territorial or having any association with the military.

Taking the appropriate route, Edgar volunteered. There is little doubt that his offer of service was prized, not because he, Edgar Mobbs had offered his service, it went far deeper than that. If, after being accepted he was simply posted to a training camp along with other Kitchener men, then his true value would have been wasted. All the records indicate that Edgar Mobbs was to be used to swell the recruiting numbers in the town of Northampton.

The Northampton papers quickly recorded that Edgar Mobbs had joined the Army as a private soldier, there is little doubt that this was to remind the 'shirkers' that it was their duty to offer their services.

It was during this time that Edgar was in correspondence with a General. These were very strange times. Even so, the demands of a nation at war had not dispelled all social convention and for a private soldier writing to a General, that was beyond all the limits of military etiquette. Was it because

THE MOBBS' OWN

he had been promised a commission and that commission should lay in abeyance until such times as the recruiting figures had been met?

Edgar with his usual outgoing and friendly personality announced that he wished to address the crowd after the next home game at the Saints, the venue of course, being the same as it is today, Franklin's Gardens.

That Saturday afternoon was one of great excitement, the casuals joined the regular fans and many young ladies attended, it was an excellent gate and not a great deal of notice was taken of the game.

After the match the crowds stayed where they were, they all wanted to listen to Edgar, who appeared before them wearing his immaculate straw boater, which was very much the fashion of the young gentlemen of the time. The speech was not long, Edgar relied on a simple direct approach. Perhaps he had in mind that the men had been saturated with the appeal for recruits. He announced simply that he was due to go to the recruiting office the following Monday, ignoring the fact, that he himself had already joined. He wanted as many as his friends and comrades to go with him. It was their chance to form their own corps and serve together. He asked them to raise their hands and indicate who was willing to join that coming Monday.

It was an amazing scene, well over two hundred men raised their hands. In many circumstances what else could they do? If you were young and healthy and possibly having the young lady you loved standing by your side, how could you possibly not raise your hand? Failure to do so was the mark of the coward. The only exceptions would be for men working in essential industry for the war effort, or those that had volunteered and had been rejected. Many of the men who raised their hands were married. This alone did not deter them, the sight of Edgar Mobbs rousing their patriotic spirits was enough. The general feeling was that these men could leave that arena at that very moment and beat the Hun.

THE MOBBS' OWN

There was much cheering and singing, straw boaters flew into the air, it was a joyous occasion for all present. As far as the recruiting committee was concerned it was their major event, and from then on the Borough of Northampton had one of the highest recruiting percentages in the entire Kingdom, an historic fact that deserves mention.

The following Monday many of the men who had been at the game and who had shown their willingness, attended the recruiting office, and from that time the Mobbs' corps was effectively formed.

It was not sufficient for this particular recruiting campaign to be confined to Franklin's Gardens. It quickly became noticed by the national press and the Saints Rugby Club took an official interest, wishing to be associated with the Mobbs' corps.

A meeting was called for present and past players by the Northants Rugby Union, this meeting to be held at the Plough Hotel. The aim was twofold, one to assist Mr.E.R.Mobbs in the forming of a local corps and secondly to cancel all further competitive games.

Mr. Fred Tyler the President of the Union was in the chair, accompanied by Mr. W.E.Billingham (chairman), Mr. J.W.Langley (hon. treasurer), Mr. W.E.Roberts (hon. secretary) and Mr.J.Watson who represented the committee. Over fifty young men made up the gathering.

The first business on the agenda was quickly dealt with, that was to endorse the action that the N.R.U. executive had made in cancelling all competitive matches for that season. The President in his address remarked.that he was glad to hear that the corps was practically formed. He had no doubt that the 'Jimmies' would make good 'Tommies' and would be worthy of the name. He considered that it was right that Rugby footballers should be called together to help old England. He approved the action of the committee and trusted that it would be an example to others. He was himself, a true sport, but he could not see how young men

THE MOBBS' OWN

could play games while England was fighting for her existence.

Edgar Mobbs was invited to speak and was received with applause. His speech was brief. Referring to Lord Robert's words, Edgar, reiterated that it was the time for deeds and not words. Every man between the ages of 19 and 35 should come to the assistance of the Empire. He announced with some pride that he already had over 250 men, and would like that number to grow to three hundred. He mentioned that pay and conditions would be announced later, but he added that he did not think pay was the question as much as how to get out there. They were not going for commissions, but were all going as Tommies with only one aim, and that was to serve the country. If they were accepted for service, and had the chance to come back again, and he hoped they would, he thought that their parents would agree they had done something to uphold the name of the good old town of Northampton.

Mr.J.Watson then added his official blessing to the meeting and moved a resolution. He wished it to be placed on record the club's appreciation of the efforts made by Mr.E.R.Mobbs in this time of great crisis, and the Northants Rugby Union hopes that every footballer who is able to do so will join, and wished the best of luck to the corps when on service.

This resolution was seconded by Mr.W.J.Stanton who added that he thought he was too old to join , but he had a son who was putting his name down.

Speaking on behalf of all the officials of the Union, Mr.W.E.Billingham, expressed with satisfaction what Mr.Mobbs had been doing. The only regret that they all had was that they were too old to join.

Lastly Mr.Tyler spoke and wished all the men that were going the best of luck. He promised that he would do all he could to assist any dependants who would be left behind.

Once again the patriotic appeals, and exuberance of Edgar

23

THE MOBBS' OWN

Mobbs had its effect, many of the young men in the gathering gave in their names to join the Mobbs' Corps.

Edgar was informed that because the Northamptonshire Regiment was full, his corps would be allocated to the Bedfordshire Regiment. It could have been a connection with Edgar's old school. In a very short time this order was rescinded and it was stated that the corps would become part of the 7th Service Battalion of The Northamptonshire Regiment and the men who had volunteered under the leadership of Edgar Mobbs would form 'D' company of that battalion. The rest of the battalion, which would be 'A', 'B' and 'C' companies would be filled from the residue of volunteers from Northampton, Corby, Wellingborough and Kettering. These men would have volunteered their service without the expressed desire of joining Edgar Mobbs.

Because of the action undertaken by the Northants Rugby club, many stars from the world of Rugby football came to Northampton and joined the Mobb's corps, showing a preference to serve with men of their own ilk.

Most of the professional and business names in the town gave their sons, all joining as private soldiers. Indeed, at this time 'D' company represented the most influential men of the town through the service of their sons.

Once again the problems of fitness had to be considered, even though 'D' company was made up from sportsmen and men from, what could only be considered, as good homes. Edgar Mobbs had amassed 400 men, which was half an infantry battalion in numbers. From this original 400, 264 men were accepted, the others failing as unfit for military duties. The following men were now enlisted:

W.H.Farrer, J.G.Rawson, F.G.Kyle, F.J.Bird, I.Shaw, S.Adams, J.R.Robinson, A.Bull, C.B.Fitch, L.W.Letts, E.Carr, A.J.Odell, W.E.Brown, A.G.Douglas, G.Blunt, D.Phillips, N.R.Spencer Robb, C.F.Dunkley, Stewart Greeves, L.E.Fitzpatrick, P.P.Perry, L.J.Roberts, A.G.Smith, P.J.Bolesworth, M.F.Turner, E.W.Buswell, W.Crick,

THE MOBBS' OWN

H.Featherstone, W.Nichols, F.Hoddle, E.C.Cocker, P.Powell, H.G.House, R.G.Cleaver, C.MCculfagh, F.Butcher, J.Warwick, C.Gayton, H.Pettit, W.E.Wilford, N.I.Tervey, J.Eldred, W.Swann, F.J.Ashton, W.G.Brown, E.A.Berresford, W.Hunt, E.Amos, A.W.Oxley, R.Sturgess, F.Winteringham, H.Mason, A.Fisher, J.N.K.Shepperd, J.Wilson, J.W.King, S.J.Hollies, W.Wooding, G.Simmons, W.J.Wheat, G.E.Foster, E.V.Mann, R.Richardson, F.E.Watkins, L.J.Dunkley, F.A.Heap, W.T.Horn, A.C.Holder, F.D.S.Lodge, G.Horton, J.S.Bailey, C.Green, G.Farey, C.Bament, H.Foreman, R.E.Stewart, G.Farr, A.M.Rushton, H.Ayris, H.K.Rowe, F.Bailey, A.H.Hawes, A.L.Bond, A.F.Betts, A.E.Allibone, F.Jeyes, W.E.Mead, W.J.Simons, F.North, W.Butcher, A.G.Whitmee, H.Sedgewick, F.A.Oliffe, W.E.Swallow, J.R.A.Willey, J.Harding, R.Corbett, R.C.Mynard, F.W.Burton, P.J.Faulkner, S.J.Smith, H.E.Hobbs, R.Hilton, F.Booth, G.Perkins, A.Tarlton, A.R.Shepherd, S.Percival, R.Pearson, C.La Hive, J.G.Gillam, T.Jones, J.Macalister, J.W.Peggs, W.Walker, A.Luck, A.Forskett, T.B.Gallantry, K.D.Allan, A.Williams, C.P.Philpot, W.B.Bennett, R.E.Gilbert, F.Payne, F.Tarry, J.Edmunds, E.H.Carter, W.A.Lee, A.Hill, S.Rice, J.C.Binyon, F.E.V.Paine, C.H.Workman, H.W.Bruce, F.R.S.Adams, W.A.Jackson, J.Stock, F.T.Allen, A.C.D.Page, W.R.Westcombe, T.S.Maddock, E.Gordon, S.F.Robins, W.H.Mundin, F.Smith, L.Skempton, B.L.Church, R.E.Rushton, D.Moore, F.Simpson, W.F.Hirons, A.T.Robertson, G.Weesle, F.J.Osborn, W.H.Tuckey, K.L.Osborn, F.Hobson, J.G.Stevens, F.E.Adkins, O.C.Wing, S.J.Westley, P.S.Merry, F.Ward, P.E.Facer, C.W.B.Smith, P.W.Facer, S.G.Bedford, E.J.Stringer, E.Squires, E.R.Odell, H.J.Williamson, W.J.C.Hebbert, C.H.BellChambers, G.Wright, L.M.Head, F.C.Deason, A.Newman, N.S.Needham, A.W.Osborn, W.Cotton, P.Foster, S.C.Wllby, J.S.Hamming, C.Marriott, W.Harris, T.Gilbert, S.Symonds, J.H.Rush, J.Looms, G.C.Davies, A.B.Carter, T.Twist, A.J.Carter, R.Dickens, T.Gibbons, J.H.Martin, R.Negrand, H.A.Main, E.W.Deeley, H.Aftleck, R.W.North, V.R.Allinson,

THE MOBBS' OWN

E.G.Butcher, C.H.Dimblebee, H.W.Brown, H.Pebody, R.Copson, E.L.C.Perry, E.F.Charles, C.T.Vernon, W.Marriott, A.E.Munroe, A.Addington, C.J.Wharmby, W.E.Howes, P.Stanton, F.W.Bass, F.H.Axford, M.I.F.Turner, F.Rowell, E.A.Cleaver, S.C.Forscutt, E.G.Crisp, A.T.Bray, A.E.Broughton, F.Totin, W.Smart, J.H.Smith, H.Willett, A.Otes, P.Tomlin, C.Trasler, A.J.Wilkinson, S.P. Garrett, H.W.Taylor, V.M.Cotton, W.H.Hammond, A.E.Justice, H.W.Redhead, E.T.Johnson, E.A.Goosey, F.Kilborn, W.R.Ashwell, P.G.Beale, J.Titley, S.Wood, F.J.Smith, F.R.W.Berry, F.W.Cracknell, F.Bridgeman, H.Grierson, J.F.Lawson, R.Tratt, A.T.Bennett, G.Green, R.L.Howell, H.Randall, J.E.Fancourt, L.Dudbridge, W.H.Munks, J.Waters, R.Bland, T.F.Manning, H.E.Hemmings.

The system arranged for volunteers was a simple one, once they had received the King's shilling and passed their medicals they would be sent home to await further orders. The Northamptonshire Regimental depot, housed in the barracks and under the command of Colonel Fawcett, could not accommodate the new service battalions. They would not be trained in Northampton but would be posted to training camps throughout the country.

One of Edgar Mobbs strongest attributes was his ability as an administrator. From his company's show room in Sheep Street, he issued duplicated letters to all the men that had joined him. In this letter he suggested what kit they should have ready, which included knives and forks, mugs, towels, a strong pair of spare trousers and blankets. Having taken the advice of Colonel Fawcett he also suggested that each man should have a spare pair of stout boots, and plenty of thick socks. This came about by Colonel Fawcett advising Edgar that a battalion shows its worth by the number of miles they can march.

The time soon came for the corps to assemble at the Northampton barracks and travel to Shoreham, in Sussex, to commence their training as a battalion.

This was a joyous day for Northampton. The Mayor had

THE MOBBS' OWN

agreed to issue the men with their first week's Army pay, accompanied by a hearty handshake. It was certainly a time for heroes. Their war was exiting, full of potential adventure and they laughed a joked in their high spirits, most of them wearing their straw boaters and others wearing sporty peaked caps. The gentlemen of the corps had sent their luggage down to the Castle Station in advance. This was done for good reason, as the corps had been invited to march down to the station, so that the local inhabitants would have the opportunity to wave and cheer them on. It was certainly good for the recruiting committee.

Even though this day was a Saturday the children from St. George's school, which was very close to the barracks, all attended and were issued with small national flags. They lined up in the Barrack Road, waiting for their strange looking soldiers to leave from the barrack gates.

A cadre of regular soldiers was in attendance and spent some agonizing moments attempting to get the corps into some type of order. The town band was in attendance and would lead the march to the station.

Thousands lined the route and became exited as the band approached them. Behind the band was the tall and erect figure of Edgar Mobbs, who gladly acknowledged the reception given by the crowds. Behind him in ragged ranks were his men. Many young ladies, some of them wives, or sweethearts, waited at the station with sprigs of heather, with which to adorn their loved ones. There were tears and laughter as they waited for their men to embark upon the special troop train that was waiting for them.

There is little doubt that the most forceful, energetic and outspoken member of the recruiting committee was one W. H. Holloway. This man's influence was immense, mainly due to the fact that he was the proprietor of the 'Northampton Independent.' Using the medium of his paper, he attacked the shirkers and the malingerers, never faltering in his insatiable desire to obtain recruits. His comments on the Mobbs' Corps

THE MOBBS' OWN

leaving for Shoreham are worth of repeat:

'The sight of Mr. Mobbs' corps of recruits marching from the homes so dear to them, was a stirring and splendid example of the spirit which animated the best of our young manhood. They have left their situations and the comforts of home, conscious that in this hour of our national peril it is the paramount duty of the young and strong in crushing the monster of brutal militarism threatening our shores. This is the traditional spirit which had made England great and free and happy and whatever Mr. Mobbs and his men have to endure for our sake, they may rest assured that they will for ever stand high in our respect and admiration for the part they are so cheerfully taking in protecting our beloved country.

> ' If anything were needed to strengthen our sense of the the brutal purposes of the Kaiser towards the British is supplied in full by the following, which the War Office intend to placard all over England.
>
> ' Latest orders from the Kaiser to his Generals.
>
> ' It is my royal and personal command that you concentrate your energies for the immediate present, upon one single purpose, and that is that you address all your skill and all the valour of my soldiers to exterminate first the treacherous English army, and walk over General French's contemptible little army.'

From that time on the veterans of the BEF were called the 'Old Contemptibles', and many gravestones of men who died in their beds, mostly in old age, bear this proud title after their names. There would have been mixed thoughts in the minds of the volunteers as they left Northampton. Their type of world had finished for the duration of the war, they were now soldiers and had little idea of what was to befall them.

THE MOBBS' OWN

Battalion on parade before the issue of clothing

The first Monday's dinner, Shoreham, 1914

THE MOBBS' OWN

The cookhouse, Buckingham Park, Shoreham, 1914

Dinner time at Shoreham, 1914

THE MOBBS' OWN

The first pay day, Shoreham, 1914

Blue emergency uniform

THE MOBBS' OWN

Detachment on beach rifle range, Shoreham, 1914

The Battalion Band

THE MOBBS' OWN

24th Division Rugby Football Team 1914 - 1915

THE MOBBS' OWN

The Battalion on Parade

THE MOBBS' OWN

Private Frank Butcher of A Company,
one of the lost generation,
killed by a mortar bomb, 15th Octobr 1915.

THE MOBBS' OWN

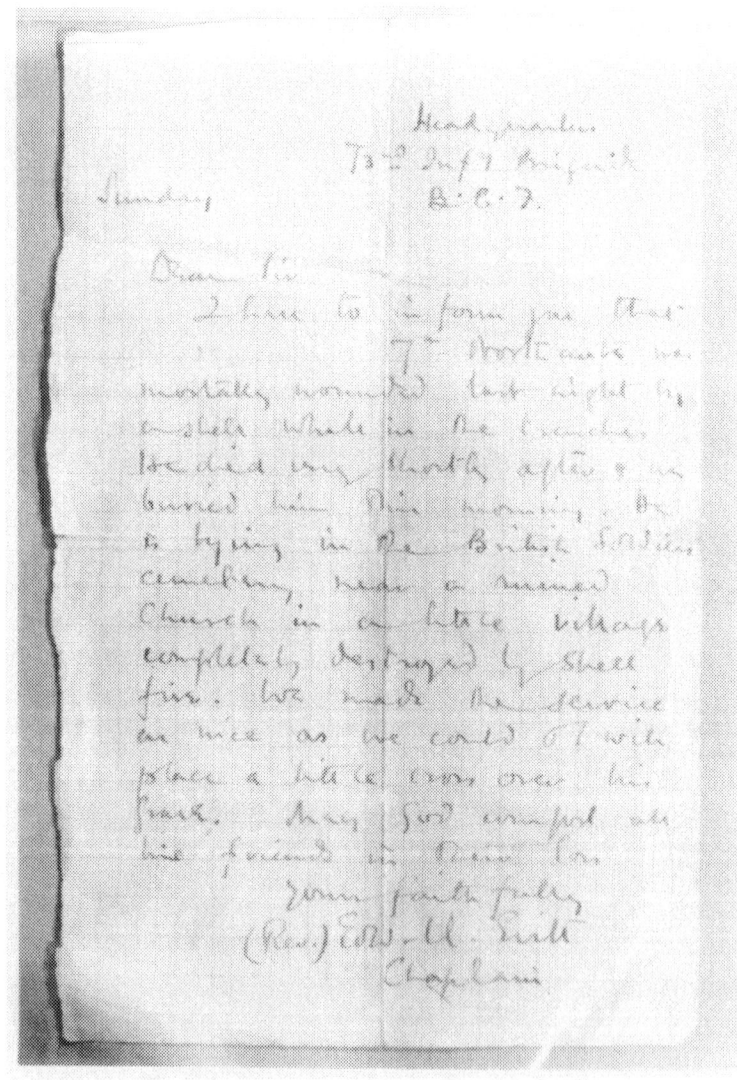

*The first tragic news for the Butcher family.
An overworked Brigade Chaplain compounded the tragedy
by leaving out Frank Butcher's name.*

Two

The Mobb's own corps, once they had arrived at Shoreham, found very little to their advantage. The reasons for this were many. A department was made responsible for quartering the troops, the Directorate of Supplies and Quartering in the Quartermasters General's Department. As Lord Kitchener and his recruiting committees fed the nation with numerous recruits, the task of quartering became close to impossible. There had been no ceiling placed on recruitment with the result that depots and training centres were not prepared for this influx of recruits.

The Corps was advised that it would belong to the 24th division and that other recruits would be arriving to form the 7th battalion.

Bell tents were ready to be assembled on the camp site which was very close to the sea and subject to strong breezes. The men found they would have to sleep up to fifteen to a tent and it was decided that the limited room could be best maximised by men sleeping with their feet towards the centre pole of the ground space.

There was one erected building in the camp, this was to be used as the orderly room and the cookhouse. There were plans to replace the tents with wooden huts and it was obvious to all that this would take time.

The men amused themselves by sea bathing, to keep clean, and pits had to be dug for sanitary reasons. To the Army these areas were labelled as foul ground. A good battalion being received by another always made it perfectly clear where their foul ground had been, otherwise the incoming battalion could bivouac on this ground with unpleasant results.

THE MOBBS' OWN

Other men arrived and it was soon discovered that these men who would make up 'A', 'B'and 'C' companies were less fortunate than the men under Edgar Mobbs. They had not been advised to bring along their own private equipment with the result that they were going to have a miserable time. To start with some boisterous iron ore miners from Corby decided to take over the tents, made reasonably comfortable by the now settled 'D' company. After some threats of fisticuffs the problem was soon solved.

Because of the lack of supplies, the cooks could produce one menu only and that was stew. The men from the other companies did not have plates. They queued for their stew with newspaper, only to see this warm and watery food, seep through and fall onto their boots.

What was crucially needed at the camp was a chain of command, for both direction and discipline. There were some 650 men, without equipment, uniforms or even a simple training scheme.

One officer did arrive to take command of the 7th battalion, until such time as the War Office could supply further officers of a mixed and varied experience. This officer was Captain Guy Paget, who made his appearance by riding a white horse and was wearing the uniform of an officer of the Scot's Guards.

There had been a write up in the Independent in regard to Captain Paget offering his service on returning to the Army. Captain Paget had been abroad when the war commenced and he immediately offered his services to return to the Scot's Guards, where, as a younger man he had been a lieutenant before resigning his commission. This was not uncommon for young gentleman from the landed gentry. The Guard's Brigade or crack cavalry regiments offered them a good social life and if, in time, they discovered that soldiering was not for them, then they could resign and return to their civilian life.

The Pagets' country seat was at Sulby Hall and both the staff and the Hall were placed at the disposal of the authorities

THE MOBBS' OWN

to be used as a convalescent home, and to defray the expense of nursing the sick and wounded who would be sent there.

Guy Paget had been abroad because of the poor health of his wife. He removed her from France and sent her to neutral Switzerland before returning to resume a military life. He was now made an acting Captain and found himself in charge of the 7th battalion Northamptonshire Regiment composed of untried men. It was a far cry from the Scot's Guards.

Paget advised Edgar Mobbs that he was promoted to a warrant officer second class, better known as a Company Sergeant Major. This must have come as a complete surprise to Edgar who had an abject ignorance of rank and its attendant responsibilities. It was true that with his natural flair for leadership, Edgar could contain his own men, to do it with rank was another matter which he was not pleased with.

To compose a command structure it was decided to select suitable men from among the recruits. As there were no uniforms, there were no badges of rank and it would be difficult for men to be recognised or acknowledged as NCO's. For reasons unknown, there happened to be a collection of coloured ribbons in the camp and these were made full use of. It was decided that Edgar would wear a yellow ribbon around his sleeve denoting his rank of a Sergeant Major. Further men were selected to be sergeants and they in their turn would wear green ribbons. Full corporals were men who had some previous service and had been awarded campaign medals and these were awarded blue ribbons. Then there came the problem of lance corporals and it was decided that the men who had fully qualified as Boy Scouts could step forward for such promotions. The promotions were as follows:

To become sergeants: F.Hobson, J.Stock, H.Pettit, C.H.Martyn, P.P.Perry, F.G.Weller and W.Ormrod. To become lance sergeants: F.T.Allen and F.Booth.

To become corporals: H.Afflick, C.T.Vernon, F.Gaynes, W.J.C.Hibbert, F.E.Adkins, T.S.Maddocks, W.Crick, R.Dickens, H.R.Simpson and M.Ruston.

39

THE MOBBS' OWN

To become lance corporals: R.E.Rushton, L.Dudbridge, S.Percival, E.W.Buswell, W.G.Brown, E.V.Mann, F.Ormrod, H.Ayres, A.F.Betts, J.H.Harding, R.L.Howett and F.D.S.Lodge.

These promotions were made within the battalion and not exclusively 'D' company, in which case Edgar Mobbs found himself to be the sergeant major over the battalion. As all soldiers will know, to become a warrant officer takes time and service. The peculiarities of words of command and the process and procedures required to follow King's Regulations and to follow the hidden code of the Army in regard to behaviour and the resulting discipline is impossible to learn within a few days and Edgar suffered as a result. If on parade an officer tells the Sergeant Major to dismiss the men, the word of command would be: Officer on parade dismiss!. In Edgar's case he could easily say: Off you go, chaps!

It was as well that Edgar did receive support. Sergeant Major F.Pearsons arrived at the camp together with Company Sergeant Major W.Neil and Quarter Master Sergeant J.Harbour.

With some trepidation the battalion found out that Pearson had been in the Guards' Brigade. They now had Paget as their officer commanding, supported by Pearson. Rumour soon spread and as the men, who were void of any equipment, could only undertake foot drill, in no time at all, the 7th battalion was known as the Northampton Guards by the other battalions in the brigade.

Other officers dribbled in together with NCO's. These men were mostly reservists who had been recalled and given the task of training the New Army. Guy Paget was appointed adjutant of the 7th battalion.

At long last, Edgar was pleased to welcome a commanding officer, Lieut.Colonel A. Parkins. Arthur Parkins was born in 1862 and was commissioned in the Northamptonshire Regiment in 1882. He took part in the majority of the colonial wars. At the age of fifty the Major, for that was his rank, retired from the Army. On the outbreak of the war, he, like many others was recalled and was given the command of the 7th battalion. It is ironic that a career officer has to retire and then be recalled to reach the rank of a Lieut.Colonel, a rank that had passed him during his regular career.

Even though Edgar Mobbs found his new commanding officer to be friendly and caring to all the men in the battalion, he requested to be reverted to the rank of sergeant. The position of a sergeant major requires certain characteristics, and Edgar, as a sporting gentleman had no intention of falling into this mould. Edgar's request was granted.

The men of the battalion were now feeling the weather, the autumn had commenced and the sea breezes were getting colder. On the orders of Colonel Parkins the camp was moved to a more sheltered spot in an attempt to protect the men from the cold sea breezes.

By this time the men's clothing was taking on a comical image. Boaters had their rims only and footwear was in a total state of disrepair. It was parcels that became the main economy of the battalion, parcels from home in answer to the needs and the often appeals from the men.

The needs of the men of the 7th trickled through to the Independent and W.H.Holloway lost no time in organising his appeal for blankets, to be transported to the camp at Shoreham.

This appeal was made on the 19th October and a total of 300 blankets was asked for. The public response was magnificent, more so when it was announced that it was now the Mayor's appeal, originating from Edgar Mobbs.

Within three days, the town had donated far more than three hundred blankets, in fact the total load weighed more than a ton weight.

The next problem presented to the town was to get the blankets to the camp. Messrs James Bros, tea provision merchants, offered their van. The journey was reported to

THE MOBBS' OWN

have been tedious and dusty by the Mayor's Sergeant who was in charge of the delivery. The following report gives a clear and viable description of what was happening at Shoreham:

'The party arrived at Shoreham at 1.40 and found a town of tents on the breezy downs with 10,000 soldiers in occupation. (It must be remembered that this was an infantry division.) It was a glorious spot, protected from the breeze by a line of trees. Two miles away the sea could be seen until it met the horizon. The health giving breezes put new vigour into the travellers, the ruddy glow of health could be seen in the faces of the members of the Northampton battalion, which Mobbs' Own form the fourth company in the battalion. Mobbs, who is soon to receive a commission welcomed us, ready hands moved the blankets from the van and the men inspected them with obvious appreciation.

> 'My impression of the 7th Northamptons were very favourable. A strong understanding was enjoyed between the men, ready for anything, clean, in the sparkle of their youth and the job set in their eyes. They have been roughing it, there was never a word of complaint, they might have been at a picnic but for the military air which pervades the place. Of hard work they have had plenty, and judging from the circumstances, it had done them good. The food is rough, but wholesome. We had a dinner in the camp, for we were treated with great hospitality by Sergeant Mobbs, to the best he could provide ham and potatoes were washed down with water in pudding basins.

Sitting on the scorched grass we eat it all with relish., though sprigs of grass and a not inconsiderable quantity of dust made its way to our plates.

> 'Soon after our arrival, the battalion now over 1,000 strong, paraded for bathing, all with towels around

their necks, making off to the sea some two and half miles away.

'The Mayor has also received some extra blankets thoughtfully subscribed by the workpeople of Messrs Hy Sharman, arranged through Miss Peel, the forewoman.

'The report of the health of the men in camp remains satisfactory, and letters we have received point to the fact that the men are hard working, but perfectly happy. The men are constantly receiving pleasant reminders of the forethought of the people at home, for Mr Salisbury, the well known tobacconist, has sent seven packets of cigarettes for each tent, and Mr.McKinnel had forwarded a pack of cards for each tent, gifts which were greatly appreciated.

'In addition to drills the men have received instructions in semaphore work and musketry and the 'D' company was taken to Lancing College, three miles away, where they were handed out rifles belonging to the O.T.C. Corps for the purpose of instruction. "An officer put us through our paces," writes a correspondent,"and though he was terribly strict the work was wonderfully interesting."

'The men have had three sea baths, which they thoroughly enjoyed. On Sunday after church parade the battalion struck camp and removed to a more sheltered spot. One recruit writing to a friend sends the following amusing paragraph: "We have a Sergeant Major. He is a devil. If you look cross eyed he wants to know the reason why."'

The recruit's reference to a sergeant major and the affliction of being crossed eyed, was no doubt, a reference to Ratty Carter.

THE MOBBS' OWN

Long retired, this Regimental Sergeant Major had returned to the Army. Ratty was a man of short temper and worked hard to make the one thousand civilians he was presented with into soldiers. Unfortunately, Ratty suffered with a squint and it was true that when he was reprimanding a soldier, no one was ever sure who was being told off. Ratty was not fit, he had been passed fit for home service only and was not expected to suffer the rigours of active service. This was not to be, for Ratty developed an affection for the 7th battalion and went with them on active service. For his gallantry he was eventually awarded the Military Cross, an award which, as a rule, is given to officers and on very rare occasion awarded to warrant officers.

Various matters can be raised by the article in connection with the blankets. The correspondent mentions that the 7th was composed of 1,000 men and yet only 300 odd blankets were taken, this also applies to the cigarettes and playing cards, all of these items were issued to 'D' Company and not shared with the battalion. There is no mention of any officer meeting the party and welcoming them, only a sergeant, who was Edgar Mobbs.

This was not missed by the people of Northampton and heated correspondence was published in the local papers. The main and obvious issue being that 'D' company was not the 7th Battalion and there were plenty of men outside of that company who needed blankets. It was also felt that most of the men in 'D' company came from wealthy families who could easily provide for their men, and it was the working class lads who deserved the support.

> The Independent was incensed by this reaction, to such an extent that Mr Holloway felt 'That these anonymous scribes who hid under the cowardly cover of anonymity, have been shooting poisoned arrows through the press in letters criticising those who are doing good work during this present crisis, deserve to be treated as enemies and put into

THE MOBBS' OWN

concentration camps until the war is over. The spirit of these scribes is not only antisocial but antinational.'

In fairness to the Independent, it would have been difficult to collect 1,000 blankets, and business people were free to give gifts to the soldiers of their choice, which in this case was 'D' company.

The writer of the article also mentioned 'D' company practising arms that belonged to a local college that possessed an O.T.C. In these early days most public schools had their own Officer Training Corps. What is not mentioned was the fact that the 7th battalion had been issued with wooden cutout rifles which were as harmless as a child's toy, but at least,they could now progress in arms drill. It was to Ratty Carter's abject horror that he discovered that these rifles were being used as line props for the mens' washing.

Because of the lack of uniforms and the disrepair of the mens' clothing, the Army decided to issue clothing called 'Kitchener's Blues.' This was composed of a jacket and trousers and side cap, at least regimental buttons were issued and the regimental badge. There was a simple reason for this design to be introduced. The dye that resulted in a khaki colour was manufactured in Germany, with a consequence that the Army had no uniforms of a regulation nature and the blue cloth was issued to compensate. In some camps the Kitchener men had been wearing the scarlet tunics of the Victorian era, at least the 7th were spared that.

The good spirits of these men were reflected in their ribaldry over these uniforms. Comments upon meeting each other were devoted to the question: ' How long have you got?' Indeed, they all looked rather like convicts and some were even taken as refugees from the continent and the town's people expressed their concern over them.

Not to be outdone by the generosity of the Northampton people, Messrs Sears the boot manufacturer presented fifty

45

THE MOBBS' OWN

pairs of brown boots to 'D' company. The managing director of that company went down to Shoreham to present them.

It is true that at this time the 7th battalion were hardly dressed the same as the regular battalions. The fact remained that only officers could wear brown boots apart from the regimental sergeant major. Edgar Mobbs must have had a problem in selecting the recipients of these boots, perhaps selecting the men who would be eventually commissioned.

In time the battalion were issued with khaki uniforms, webbing and arms. At long last the 7th appeared to be part of the British Army.

Captain Guy Paget had abandoned his Scot's Guards regalia and had adopted the collar dogs and cap badge of the Northamptonshire regiment, and this applied to all, irrespective of their previous regiments.

The generosity of the town persuaded Captain Paget to make an appeal, this being the first occasion where an officer had undertaken such a request.

The Indepenent had been running a cigarette fund for the county regiment and following up this donation, Guy Paget wrote to the indefatigable editor W.H.Holloway. His letter was a follows:

> 'The success of your Cigarette fund for the County Regiment encourages me to ask whether you would mind getting a few drums, fifes and bugles for the Battalion. Probably many of your readers have them, but never use them. It really only requires looking up and a bit of trouble, which I know the ' Independent' never grudges in a good cause.'

It is worthy of mention that in the victory honours Mr. Holloway was awarded the Order Of The British Empire for his work with recruiting and relationship with the Army.

Mr.Holloway took up this challenge and published his appeal: 'I have much pleasure in giving publicity to this appeal in the confident belief that my readers will make an adequate response, as they have always have done to any call we have made upon their generosity. As I fear there may not be sufficient instruments in disuse among my readers for this purpose I have opened a fund for buying a new set. Everyone of the few friends I have privately asked has readily promised to be responsible for a drum, bugle or fife. Mr.A.Gilbert Whitlock has kindly offered to supply them at cost price, so that each subscriber of one guinea will furnish a drum, twelve and six a bugle, half a crown a fife. The name and address of each subscriber will be attached to each instrument so that the battalion band may know who are their benefactors. A list of contributors, but not the amounts, will be published in this paper. There are several good instrumentalists in the battalion, and I am sure there are sufficient good friends among our readers who will be ready and indeed eager to help in furnishing our patriotic sons at Shoreham with this practical proof of our appreciation, which will also enliven their life in the camp and the monotony of their musicless marches. Will intending subscribers kindly send their contributions without delay to the Editor of the 'Northampton Independent', 14 Guildhall Road, Northampton, as we want to get the collection of instruments by the end of next week.'

This appeal was a great success, showing that the influence of Edgar Mobbs had made the 7th battalion the talking point of the town. At much later dates other service battalions did receive band equipment from the town, but it was the Mobbs' battalion that were the instigators and without their local hero, the battalion would have been just another extension to the regiment.

The Northampton people could not ignore the 7th battalion and the response was instant and Holloway was eager to tell the town about the result:

'Last week Capt. and Adjutant Guy Paget of the 7th Northamptonshire Regiment at Shoreham camp, asked me to appeal to my readers for a few drums, fifes and bugles for the battalion. The response was remarkable.

THE MOBBS' OWN

Within a day I had more than sufficient promises to equip them with a brand new set of instruments, and I must express my grateful thanks on behalf of the battalion to those ladies and gentlemen who so gladly subscribed. The instruments are being dispatched to the camp at Shoreham in a few days, and it will, I feel sure, help to relieve the monotony of their long marches and life in camp. The spirit with which the donors subscribed will make the gift of the band all the more welcome to the battalion. Mr.H.B.Spurgin, who was Lieut. Colonel in the 3rd Northamptonshire Regiment, in subscribing for a drum wrote:

'Dear Sir,

I am sorry I am not a proud possessor of a drum, fife or bugle to send you, but I have much pleasure in enclosing you a cheque for a guinea towards the musical instruments of the 7th Northamptonshire Regiment. I think marching without a band is very dull work, and it strikes me as odd that the Division at present with us cannot raise one between them.

Believe me,

Yours truly,

H.B.Spurgin.

'After subscribing for a drum (Mr.F.Tyler) added: "I hope it will be well beaten like the Germans."

'With a remittance for a bugle Mr.R.Knight of Oundle said: "I gladly subscribe for a bugle because I am certain it will be always blown in charge for right against might."

'Not being a bandsman myself I have forgotten to appeal for the chief instrument of them all, and wondering whom I could 'Tap' for a big drum , when strange to say, I received a delightful surprise from Mrs.Langton of Tenton House, who kindly wrote offering not only a large drum, but a small one, several fifes, music and attachments. Another generous offer was contained in the following letter:

Dear Sir,

In reference to your appeal in the 'Independent,' for instruments for the 7th battalion Northamptonshire Regiment, we have much pleasure in handing you herewith 12 flutes (6 four keyed and 6 one keyed) which are suitable for drums and fife bands.

Yours faithfully,

Abel and Sons.

Colonel Fawcett of the Northamptonshire's depot wrote his own letter in response and thanked all the donors in the town.

It was true that the 7th battalion was held in high regard by the town of Northampton. In one sense the battalion had been raised by the town, starting with its own hero Edgar Mobbs. No man at that time could have achieved the same success. There was a combination of patriotism, civic pride and the desire to contribute towards the welfare of the battalion. The main weakness being the constant interest in 'D' company, who proudly held the distinction of being called "Mobbs' Own".

Now the battalion was involved in acceptable military training, having been equipped as a regular unit, it was decided that promotions should be pursued. It was an excellent ploy for the establishment to accept educated young men and allow them to serve as privates, for this, in its own way persuaded working class lads to join the colours. Now came the time to commission the gentlemen. Later in the war, the French army was in mutiny because of the dreadful losses they suffered, having to be sacrificed by the elan pursuits of their generals. The one simple, if not tragic way, the British

THE MOBBS' OWN

Army retained discipline was the constant loss of young officers.

These young men were expected to lead their platoons into the open spaces of no man's land, wearing the distinctive service dress and Sam Browne belt, favoured by British officers. In mortal combat, soldiers are trained to eliminate the leaders of the enemy and a young subaltern was not allowed to disguise his rank. The average length of service in the infantry for a newly commissioned officer, once having commenced active service, was six weeks. Many men from the ranks who had proved themselves as excellent soldiers, refused commissions that were offered to them.

Edgar Mobbs was at last commissioned, not with the one star of a second lieutenant, but the two stars of a full lieutenant, thereby not being placed in a probationary rank. There is no doubt that he had proved his worth and indeed was excellent officer material, his leadership quality was evident in the manner that he had built up his own company of volunteers.

The promotions did not stop with Edgar Mobbs. No fewer than 36 members of the battalion were granted commissions, and this was claimed as a record for the British Army.

Some of the men commissioned stayed with the 7th battalion, their names were as follows:

D.H.Farrar, H.Grierson, C.H.Martyn, R.L.Howett, S.Percival and E.G.Butcher.

Because of a shortage of officers within the New Army, the following men, having been commissioned from the ranks, were posted to the regiments or battalions as designated:

B.L.Church and N.J.Darling to the 4th Northamptons,

R.G.Duchesne, H.C.F.Shepherd, D.Winteringham, A.C.D.Page and G.D.Spearing, to the 8th Northamptons,

G.E.Foster, M.F.Turner to the 2nd Monmouths,

H.B.Simpson to the 6th Northamptons,

F.G.Weller, to the 10th Bedfords,

THE MOBBS' OWN

W.E.Robb, to the A.S.C.,
E.M.Harrison to the 8th Lincolns.
P.P.Perry to the Shropshire Light Infantry,
W.C.Hibbert, to the 10th King's Own R.L.R,
E.G.Crisp to the 15th Warwickshire Regiment,
R.Dickson to the 13th Sherwood Foresters,
L.Skempton to the 3rd South Staffs,
I.Dudbridge to the 5th Gloucesters,
H.W.Bruce, to the 11th Black Watch,
A.H.Dawes, to the 5th Leicestershires,
T.R.W.Berry, to the 10th Sussex,
A.J.Martin, to the 3rd South Staffs,
R.G.Smithers (Regiment not recorded),
K.D.Allen to the Royal Engineers,
W.R.Ashwell to the 5th Leicestershires,
G.Horton, to the 22nd Middlesex and C.B.Hornby, to the Shropshire Light Infantry, where he was accidentally killed.

It can be readily seen that the number of service battalions was dependent upon the size of the county. One of these men going to the 15th Warwickshires and another going to the 22nd Middlesex which, in actual fact was a huge regiment due to its recruiting area. Once again, this brings to mind, the struggle the Northamptonshire recruiting committee had in keeping its ten battalions up to strength. Once these battalions entered upon active service and suffered losses, it was found that it had to be totally replaced in just over a year, which was a great strain upon the county's manpower.

To further the course of recruiting, Edgar Mobbs returned to Northampton, this time bringing his own Rugby team from the battalion.

There was to be an Military International match at the county ground. The funds accrued from the match would be given to the Mayor's War Funds. J.B.Minihan the Hon.Sec.

THE MOBBS' OWN

East Midlands R.U. had arranged this game, and true to form the Independent gave this full coverage:

> 'The following interesting letter with reference to the Military International match, which is expected to attract a large attendance at the County Ground tomorrow (Saturday) had been received from J.B.Minihan, who was responsible for the management of the fixture:
>
> " Dear Sir May I ask you to give special prominence to the Military Rugby International match that takes place at the County Ground on Saturday. I have long desired to do something from a "Rugger" point of view to assist the war funds, but as nearly 90 per cent of our men have answered their country's call, I found the greatest difficulty in arranging a first class game. However, the military exigencies of the moment gave me my chance and was able to induce Lieut. Mobbs to bring his XV down to meet Lieut. Ian Pender's Scotch side from Bedford and Kettering. Both are powerful teams and a very fine game should result. The object I had in view was to assist the Mayor in forming a local war relief fund for his use in necessitous cases, and trust the gate will be sufficiently large to enable him to make a grant towards the fund, organised by the Northampton Independent, for sending smokes and comforts to our brave soldiers at the front. I have been promised a regimental pipers band, who will accompany the team and its supporters who intend to travel by the special excursion arriving Midland's Railway station at 1.45 p.m. They will play through the streets en route to the County Ground and also give selections before the match. Lieut. Edgar Mobbs had written to me, saying that he will bring his team down to Northampton Friday

THE MOBBS' OWN

evening and adds that they are all in strict training and hope to put up a fine game and win. Lieut. Ian Pender (last years Scottish International) has been very successful in collecting a fine side, but his men have not had the same chance as our old skipper's men in getting together and practising often. This is their only handicap.

"Everything points to a rare match, and given good weather we should have a great day and a rush for the recruiting officer. There are still many vacancies in the 7th battalion Northant's Regiment, and I am desired by Lieut. Mobbs to say that he will be glad to see any young fellow in the dressing room after the match with a view to enlisting."

The weather was tolerable on that February day in Northampton and Edgar's boys won their match. There is no record to say how many recruits he obtained, any young man who wished to visit the star of the day would be expected to show a firm commitment to volunteer for the 7th.

As a point of interest the Mobb's Military International was made up from the following:

Pte.S.Skempton, Corpl.Fitzpatrick, Pte.Benyon, Pte.Mann, Pte.Willet, Lance Corpl.Danbridge, Pte.Gillam, Sergt.Martyn, Pte.Lawson, Lieut.E.R.Mobbs, Lieut.Grierson, Pte.Butcher, Pte.Brookman, Second-Lieut.Gurney and Capt Holloway (Cambridge University.)

The real miracle of the event was the attendance of the band, which after such a short time together and of doubtful lineage, had the confidence to march through the town playing their marches. Humanity, in the shape of close to a thousand men can produce talent, some of it obvious, and in many cases latent.

Colonel Parking wrote to the Independent, who had been the instigators of the band, following the appeal from Captain Paget, assuring the town that they were for ever thankful for

THE MOBBS' OWN

the instruments provided.

This small band was immaculately turned out and was given a rousing reception by the town people. These men had worked very hard, their main practice taking the men down to the beach at Shoreham for their ablutions. Early reports from the men stated that some funny noises were being made by the band, but in time they improved. This must have been the case for this time they were on their first public show and it must have been both exiting and daunting for them. The instrumentalists from the 7th were as follows:

Bandmaster and Drum Major F.T.Allen. Sidedrummers, Lance Corpl.Pebody, Pte.Simons, Pte.Swallow, Lance Corpl.Blair; Drummer, Pte.Lunn, (resplendent in his tiger skin.) Buglers: Corpl.Butcher, Pte.Hall, Pte Abbott, Pte.Noon, Pte.Strickland, Pte.Butcher, Pte.Beresford, Pte.Forskitt, Pte.Fitch, Pte.Gardner. Fifers: Pte.Garner, Pte.Mann, Pte.Cotton, Pte.Hoddle, Pte.Wharmby, Pte.Smith, Pte.Hitchcock, Pte.Goodwin, Pte.Noon, Pte.Westcombe, Pte.Foreman and Pte.Brown.

The euphoric nature of the war, was now fast diminishing. By 1915 the town was already in sadness. Young wives and sweethearts would go to Castle Station waiting for the wounded to be returned from the front. They thrust photographs of their missing loved ones into the faces of these hapless men, hoping that they could give the information, which the War Office was not able to do. A man could be reported as being killed, or wounded, or missing, believed killed. It was very rare that there was an official confirmation made. Some of the men reported as being dead, turned up as prisoners of war, this also applied to men categorised as being missing. Very often families had to rely on letters sent by the officers of the mens' regiments, and due to the heat and conditions of battle,these letters could be of limited value. Each morning a casualty list was posted by the steps of the Town Hall, and women approached this list with anxiety, hoping that husbands, sons and loved ones were not included. As the war continued these lists became longer.

THE MOBBS' OWN

W.H.Holloway, being the champion of the war effort offered his usual services. He arranged appeals for food parcels to be sent to the men captured and in the early days of the war was actually engaged in correspondence with a German officer in command of one of the camps. There is little doubt that these parcels would have saved some of these mens' lives, as conditions were very poor.

A further offer made by Mr.Holloway, was in connection with the graves of the dead; if they were known. For a sum of 2/6d (12½p) a postcard photograph of a loved one's grave could be forwarded. Over 75,000 men who died in this war, have no known graves.

With the appearance of the band and Edgar Mobbs due to play at the County Ground the next day, the opportunity was taken for a recruiting meeting to be held at the Town Hall, with many important speakers. The main group were made up of the following: Capt.Rich, Sir W.D.Ryland Atkins, M.P., Coun.L.F.Cogan, Lord Hugh Cecil M.P., The Mayor (Coun.F.C.Parker.) Coun.Alfred Smith, Lieut.Desmond Chapman-Huston, Capt.Guy Paget, Major A.E.Ray, and Lieut. E.R.Mobbs.

This was a case of the local and national dignities giving their own appeals for recruits, the speakers' table being flanked by coloured double crown posters that were headed 'Rally Round The Flag.'

Because of the dwindling desire to volunteer for an Army already suffering heavy casualties, the efforts of the civilian speakers fell flat. This was not so with the officers from the military. Sir Ryland Atkins, stated that he spoke with authority. Speaking as a member of parliament, bedecked in a high winged collar and a dark formal suit this did not go down with the members of the audience who already had men serving, if not lost.

Captain Rich who had just returned from the front was given a better reception, even though he was dressed in civilian attire, including the buttoned spats of a gentleman.

55

THE MOBBS' OWN

As the Independent reported, the presence of Captain Paget and Lieutenants Chapman-Huston and E.R.Mobbs made telling points by simply being present in their uniforms.

Lord Hugh Cecil, the principal speaker, was due to speak last. He had good reason to regret this, for prior to his own address it was the turn of Edgar Mobbs. They cheered and cheered, not because he was an Army Officer but because he was their old Rugger captain, still loved by all. Edgar had to calm them down and soon had them all laughing. Lord Cecil could not understand all the fuss and light heartedness. It was obvious to him that this officer was of low rank for his age and displayed no campaign medals to denote a military career. So why all the fuss? The Mayor in his wisdom placated the noble lord, explaining quickly who Edgar Mobbs was.

Edgar told them about his career as a Sergeant Major, and what a hopeless one he was, having no idea of what he should be doing. One day an officer came to him with red all over him, and Edgar indicated that attention must be paid to an officer with this type of uniform, for he must have been important. This officer gave orders to Edgar to prepare a fatigue party of fifty men. Edgar answered, with some confusion, that he would get his men, but had no idea what a fatigue was. The frustrated officer, merely stated, no doubt looking down his nose at the same time, that Edgar, was the strangest Sergeant Major he had ever met. He departed with a kindly word, encouraging him to do his best.

Because the battalion had many men recalled from the reserves to train them, many had not been involved in military duties for many years. The 7th had an old sergeant who had been a publican and could not rid himself of calling a platoon a spitoon.

The evening finished with patriotic songs rendered by Mr.Harvey Reeves and Mr.E.R.Tapp.

It had been a happy time for the Rugger team and the band, they had been welcomed as heroes and had proved their value as a recruiting medium. The Mobb's XV won their match by

THE MOBBS' OWN

52 points to 13. In fact, the Mobb's XV during their training in England played many matches and only suffered one defeat and that was at the hands of the Barbarians. They became their Division's champion, sweeping all before them.

It was now time for 'D' company and the 7th Battalion to think of war. They had been training for a year. The vigorous training they had endured had made them sound physical specimens. Gone were the days without uniform, only to be replaced by an embarrassing substitute of blue. By this time the tents had been replaced by wooden huts and the camp was no longer just an open space, it was now a military establishment. They were a fully equipped regular battalion eager to take on the enemy.

Before leaving Shoreham further notices of promotions came down from division. Edgar Mobbs, D.H.Farrar and H.Grierson were promoted to the rank of captain. Edgar being given fourteen days seniority over his fellow captains which at a later date would have a great bearing on his military career. R.T.B.Houghton, C.L.Clarke and L.L.Phipps, were promoted to full lieutenants.

As the division was expecting orders to muster and go to France, there was some considerable excitement. All the men looked forward to active service.

The grind of constant training in the midst of a war, did not add to the morale of this division.

Orders came through and the 7th being part of the 24th division, at long last left Shoreham and headed for Chobham.

Lord Kitchener arrived at Chobham to inspect the division. He was accompanied by General Sir Archibald Hunter, General Sir John Ramsay, and General Oswald of the 73rd Brigade.

The whole of the 24th division stretched for over three miles and apart from the 7th Northamptonshires, comprised battalions of the Bedfordshire Regiment, the Buffs, Royal Norfolks, the Suffolks, Royal Fusiliers, the Middlesex and

THE MOBBS' OWN

Royal Sussex.

The prefix 'Royal' is appended to regiments who fought for Charles 1st, and Cromwellian regiments were denied this honour. As Northampton was a Cromwellian garrison for most of the civil war, the county regiment were Roundheads and as a consequence were not Royal.

After inspecting each battalion, Lord Kitchener called each commanding officer forward. With his soldier's eyes Lord Kitchener had admired the parade performance of the 7th Northamptons and congratulated Colonel Parkins on his battalion's turnout and steadfastness on parade.

Instead of embarking for France, the 7th found they were marching up the famous hill in Guildford, and by doing so, were much admired by the local inhabitants. They then proceeded to dig defences surrounding London and it was felt that digging was a much required skill for the Western Front.

On the 28th August 1915 the final orders came through, this time they would go to France.

Some of the men had already enjoyed embarkation leave, 500 men missed out on this privilege because the new orders to move out, did not allow them the time.

Major J.W.Fisher arrived to take over command of 'B' company, Captain H.Grierson assumed command of 'A' company.

Company arrangements were made to have kit inspections, and each man was fitted with a pair of field service boots, and ammunition was issued to make up the mens' combat kit.

It was then found that the recruiting committee had worked so hard, using the value of Edgar Mobbs, that the battalion was 98 men over strength, whereas most of the battalions in the division were under strength and brigade transfers were made. Ten men were transferred to the 17th Royal Fusiliers and 68 men to the 9th Royal Sussex. A few of the men in the 7th were found to be unfit and were sent back

THE MOBBS' OWN

to the depot in Northampton.

Embarking for France the 7th Service Battalion of the Northamptonshire Regiment was at an exact compliment.

Three

Why the 7th battalion together with territorial divisions and other service battalions had been called to France, was all part of a master plan. There was going to be a Franco British offensive that would, hopefully shatter the German front, and escape the stagnation of trench warfare that had become the norm on the Western Front.

General Sir Douglas Haig was in command of the 1st Army that would undertake the offensive. Haig mistrusted the plan that was presented to him. In the first place he considered that the supply of heavy artillery and shells fell far short of what he required for such an attack.

There had been a great deal of discussion over this thorny problem of shells, both in Parliament and in the national press. At Ypres faulty shells had been the cause of death for many gun crews, suffering from shells exploding in the breech, and there had been little improvement by 15th September 1915, the date the battle of Loos commenced. The figures produced at that time clearly indicated this major weakness in British production, in England the production of shells amounted to over twenty thousand a day, in France this figure was one hundred thousand and the Germans two hundred and fifty thousand.

Haig was reluctant to carry out an offensive until such time as his artillery could be built up, both in guns and shells. This was not to be allowed. Pressure from the British General Staff to comply with this plan devised by the French Generals, Joffre and Foch, made it perfectly clear that nothing was to be done to weaken the French plan. This was taken to such an extent that it was suggested that Sir John French's army should be divided so that any counter instructions from

THE MOBBS' OWN

French, could not damage the offensive.

There were to be two blows of a convergent nature at separate sectors, one at Arras Lens and the second at Reims the Argonne. The idea behind the plan, that if there was a breakthrough in these two sectors then the French and British Armies would mount a great offensive that would finish the war, by pushing the Germans beyond the Meuse.

Prior to this planned offensive Haig visited the proposed battle ground and came to a conclusion, finding that it was unsuitable for an attack. He considered two reasons, one, that the German army was present in strength and secondly the ground was too open, lacking any real type of cover for the infantry. His objections were thrust to one side by Joffre.

As this argument continued with the allied commanders, the Germans were busy in building strong defensive positions.

It was ordered that Haigs's Army should attack just north of Lens, and the unsuitability of the site or its defence should be ignored. This was further reinforced by Lord Kitchener who informed Sir John French that every assistance should be given to the French even though the Army would suffer heavy losses. Sir John French considered that he needed thirty six divisions to be effective. He was compelled to commence the offensive with nine divisions. The attack commenced after much soul searching by Haig who wanted to use chlorine gas to support his few divisions. Because of the wind direction and in some cases the lack of it, the gas was apt to drift back among the British troops who were waiting to attack.

French, as commander in chief, was responsible for the placement of his reserves. These reserves would be used to fill in gaps caused by the German counter attack, or take over ground that had been overrun by the British advance. This reserve consisted of the Cavalry Corps, which in such terrain and against such fire power was quickly proved to be useless, a consideration constantly rebuffed by French and Haig, who were cavalry officers. The rest of the reserve was made up from the Guards Division, and the 21st and 24th Divisions, the latter included the 7th battalion. These three divisions had not yet experienced active service.

The commander in chief had promised Haig that these divisions would back up his offensive. On the Somme front at this time, experienced divisions were idling their time away as nothing was really happening, and yet French preferred to bring into battle these raw, untried divisions.

General Haig's Army did break through and he required support from his reserve. He had been told that they were some sixteen miles behind the line. He quickly discovered that they were a full days march away and in spite of this ordered them to the front.

A single battalion such as the 7th can easily be lost in the events of the time. The 7th belonged to a brigade which was their immediate command under a brigadier general who commanded four service battalions. These brigades collectively would make a division, and the divisions would comprise an army.

Before the 7th battalion went into action they had already lost a man, for Private Keech had gone missing at Boulogne, was then arrested tried at a general court martial and sentenced to three months field punishment No 1. Apart from being absent his other crime was stealing a bottle of French wine.

On the 21st September the battalion left Torcy and marched for six hours to arrive at Laires at 2 a.m. There was little rest for them. They left Lairdes at 6 p.m. to join the Brigade and then undertook a nine hour march to L'Ecleme where they were allowed to rest for a day.

It must be remembered that these men were wearing full service marching order equipment, including their Lee Enfield rifles, rations, ammunition and grenades. At this time the Army had not been issued with steel helmets to add to their weight of equipment. As ironic as it may sound, Army orders gave a maximum weight that was to be carried by mules, this being no more than a third of their body weight, soldiers had to carry one half of their body weight. On the 25th September, the battalion was ordered to march to the front and occupy trenches captured by the Scottish Brigade made up by the Seaforths, Gordons and Royal Scots.

The late Percy Slarke gave a vivid description of this march into action. He mentioned the exhaustion of the men as they heard heavy shelling in the distance. As the light improved they could see the barbed wire emplacements ahead of them. Percy could see material flapping in the wind, and assumed that some of the troops must have been hanging their washing out to dry before the offensive had started. As the battalion moved closer, the grim reality became plain to see. The material flapping in the breeze was the kilts belonging to dead highlanders hanging on the wire. The cliche, a baptism of fire, could be easily used for this introduction to the reality of war, for all these young men, including Edgar Mobbs who was pushing along his 'D' company, showing his high spirit and becoming impervious to danger.

Occupying the trenches the 7th found that Scottish troops had been separated from their command and were drifting back into the trenches. The Germans counter attacked, and the 7th made up from sportsmen and cobblers and iron ore miners found they were facing the Prussian Guard. These elite soldiers with their long ankle length greatcoats were advancing across open ground as if they were on parade, and the Lewis gunners of the battalion fired off drum after drum into the advancing ranks.

The Germans wavered and fell back only to return and engage in hand to hand fighting. Edgar Mobbs rallied men around him, men from the Northamptons and the remnants of the Scots. Fixing bayonets they charged the enemy time and time again, lost in the brutality of close fighting that gives no time to think, only to act and survive.

Because of the weakness on the flanks of the battalion the Germans came in from the rear, and the battalion had to take

THE MOBBS' OWN

up firing positions on the rear of the trenches which had not been built for firing positions and failed to give adequate cover.

It had been said that Edgar Mobbs' service dress was in rags, from particles of shrapnel that tore at his uniform and somehow missed his flesh. His only wound was on the bridge of his nose.

There was no doubt that Edgar acted in a brave if not close to reckless manner, rallying troops that must have been close to collapse and ready to escape the front and the hell that must have been unbelievable. In this action Edgar should have been rewarded for his gallantry. It is a peculiarity that gallantry must be observed by a senior officer, if not, then it never happened, and therefore no recommendations would be made. The testimony of other ranks was never taken into consideration.

Crossing from one trench to another Colonel Parking was shot in the head and died instantly. In their first action the 7th had lost their commanding officer. This officer had been a fair and kindly man, tolerating his battalions slow metamorphosis from civilians to soldiers.

Captain Paget collected stragglers to be used as reinforcements. Approaching the firing a bullet passed through his left puttee and twice he was thrown into the air by shell fire, badly shaken he carried on. Yet another shell exploded close to him and this time he was knocked unconscious and buried by the debris. To all intent and purposes he had vanished. The men around him lost two men killed and several were wounded. The survivors dug frantically. Captain Paget who was also suffering from a broken rib came round to find himself face down in total darkness and could hear the voices of the men who were pulling him from his premature grave. He could clearly remember a voice saying: 'We won't leave our ******* adjutant to the Huns!'

Prior to his own wounding and just before the 7th had entered the Hohenzollern Redoubt, Captain Paget had come

THE MOBBS' OWN

across General Thesiger, who was complaining bitterly that the men were not carrying enough bombs(grenades) and Paget was ordered back with his men to get some. On his return, Paget came across the body of a staff officer and on closer inspection found that it was that of General Thesiger. It was not uncommon at that time for staff officers to be killed. It was later in the war that senior officers found it more practical to stay well behind the line.

After fierce and unremitting fighting, the 7th pulled back to a reserve trench, allowing the Germans to retake the line that had been previously won by the Highlanders.

These men had marched over 70 miles in two days. Their initial advance had been so rapid that supplies failed to come through. From late on the Saturday night to the following Monday morning, these men had no water. There were no sanitary conveniences of any type in the trenches, men who fell wounded had to lay in urine and excrement. There was no sleep or rest and the battalion was subjected to heavy shell fire. During their occupation of the first line they were never more than 30 to 60 yards from the enemy.

The 7th were pulled out of the line and were placed on a train and sent to Bergett, and from there to undertake a further 6 mile march to Norrent Fontes arriving in the early hours of the morning. At daylight they marched for 4 miles to arrive at Lambrest.

At last the 7th were allowed some rest. At this time the 7th were commanded by Major Compton who came from the 4th battalion as a temporary measure.

Clearing stations had to be contacted. These stations were responsible for taking in men separated from their battalions and making notes of the men who had been taken away as being wounded, had died of their wounds or had been killed in the offensive.

During this action, Percy Slarke who was by then a corporal, had been making an effort to get back behind the line

65

to find water tanks for the battalion and was continuously being blown over by shell fire. Some Highlanders came across him and finding that he was an NCO clung close to him. Before going to the front, all British soldiers had been warned that if they purposely broke away from their command in the heat of battle, they would be classified as cowards and shot! These Highlanders were making certain that an NCO from the 7th was legitimising their presence and there would be no charge of cowardice.

> The grim task of attempting to produce a casualty list was begun. The following few lines have been taken from the Official War Diary of the battalion: 'Casualty list prepared from information gathered from Coys. It was a first thought that some lists would be received from the various clearing stations but these did not arrive. The situation was as follows: killed 21, wounded 132, missing 204, gassed 5. This is in no way authentic.'

The 7th had been decimated. There was no authenticity because the companies could only produce information as they knew it. The figure of 21 killed could only be based on the men actually killed in the trenches. As the battalion left the trenches to counterattack then the men lost in no mans' land could not be readily identified. As the area was being constantly shelled, men who had been killed or wounded, would be either blown to pieces, or at the very least buried by debris. It could be assumed that the majority of the 204 missing would be dead.

By sheer coincidence, at this very time, the recruiting committee had organised a mass recruiting rally on the Market Square in Northampton. Over 25,000 people attended this rally. The platform being the veranda of the Peacock Hotel, was flanked by wounded soldiers with pristine bandaging, the distinguished speakers and guests, gathered. As was the usually the case, the recruiting committee was present in full force, led by Earl Spencer.

> The Mayor, Councillor F.C.Parker opened the proceedings and quickly stated that that the meeting had not merely been called for a torchlight display. 'The gentlemen on the platform had come for the purpose of obtaining recruits. Proud as they were of the voluntary spirit which had produced three million men, they were asking for more. We had got to fling the Germans outside of Flanders, outside of France and outside of Russia. The time has come when all men of military age should come forward to help those that were already fighting. We have had 8,000 men fighting with the Northampton battalions and if more men did not come forward we should not be able to take advantage of our successes. I am sure Northampton will take its part and answer the call of duty.'

This address was well received and was followed by a Naval appeal by the Hon. Rupert Guiness who held the rank of a Lieut.Commander and was asking for men to serve in the Royal Naval Division, which was a land force, fighting by the side of the Army.

Earl Spencer in his address informed the crowd that long speeches were a thing of the past. This could have been prompted by the long casualty lists that no longer allowed jingoism, the people wanted to know the truth. The Earl in his short speech attempted to get to the real issues.

> 'Men, men, always more men.' He then went on to praise the fine traditions of the regiment and said that everything should be done to produce recruits. 'The record of our regiment is a fine one . It is one that those who come after us will be proud to remember. Let me call your attention to this most potent and powerful fact . Only this day last week, last Friday and Saturday, a battalion of our great regiment was engaged in the fiercest fight that has

ever taken place in the history of the world. We are proud of them. We suffer with them, but also glory with them. I for one feel elevated and inspired by the courage, endurance and cheerfulness that all our men in all our battalions of our regiment, those who have been in action and those who are waiting to go into actions, have shown. Now I ask you to carry away from this meeting the determination to recruit, and to keep on recruiting.'

Earl Spencer had referred to the battle of Loos and the involvement of the 7th battalion. Like all in the town, Earl Spencer had no information about the 7th, or its losses. At that time there was much anxiety, the battalion had gone into action for the first time and there was no information with regard to its losses.

News did trickle through, mainly from Castle Station, where trains had been bringing in the wounded from the offensive. Among these men were a smattering of men from the Northamptons, and some letters from the front had arrived in the town. This information was gathered by the editor of the Northampton Daily Chronicle, who quickly assesses this fragmented information and arrived at his conclusions.

As it was a Saturday and there were thousands of people in the town centre due to the recruiting rally, the editor of the Daily Chronicle made full use of his late edition. He used banner headlines in his paper: '7th Northamptons Cut Up!' These same words were used on placards used by the vendors, who lost no time in shouting the very same words among the gathering on the Market Square.

This dramatic news caused chaos among the gathering crowd and negated the rally, it was certainly a poor platform to obtain recruits.

Some days afterwards, W.H.Holloway once again turned to his pen and through his medium of the Independent attacked his colleague with his usual patriotic fervour. It had been the 'Daily Chronicle' that had published their reader's letters criticizing the issue of blankets to 'D' company and there was little love between the two local editors.

There had been a law passed in Parliament, the Defence Of The Realm Act. This act prohibited the publication of material that could damage the war effort, and any perpetrators found guilty of such acts, could be faced with severe punishments, if their actions were considered to be of a treasonable nature. W.H.Holloway considered that the editor of the 'Daily Chronicle,' should be prosecuted under this act. The 'Daily Chronicle' did make an apology and as their offending headlines did have a substantial element of truth, there was no prosecution. This did not deter Holloway or his paper from making a scathing attack:

> 'The agony of anxiety which thousands of persons in town and county are suffering concerning the relatives in the 7th Northamptons was disgracefully exploited by the "Northampton Daily Chronicle" on Saturday night with flaming posters and huge headlines, boldly and brutally proclaiming: "7th NORHAMPTONS CUT UP."

> 'Newsboys flaunted the placards and shouted the terrible tidings in the crowded streets. The indiscretion of the whole business was appalling. There seemed almost an exultant element in the way the message was phrased and pushed into the faces of passersby. From a sordid standpoint the sensational trick paid, for there was a feverish rush for the papers by the panicstricken public, but the only justification they found for the alarming announcement was in a sentence in a letter sent home by a wounded soldier. We cannot blame the soldier. He was only writing of that small section of the great advance immediately around him, and we

know that wounded men are not in the best position to judge things in their proper perspective. We cannot, however, too strongly deprecate the action of any newspaper causing needless distress by giving prominence to such sensationalism. In this case the panic spread painfully. Throughout Sunday, in hundreds of homes the mental tension and the torture which was suffered would be distressing to describe. The post, next morning was awaited with a chill dread, and when there came no confirmation that the battalion had been cut up but rather that the loses were light considering the severity of the struggle, the offending journal began to have reasons to repent its rashness. Indignant expressions from those who have dear ones in the Regiment were to be heard on every side. In editorial sanctum visions doubtless began to arise of the possible enforcement of clause 27 of the Defence Of The Realm Act, which as every editor ought to know, provided that any person by word or mouth or in any printed publication spreads reports or statements likely to prejudice the recruiting,training,discipline of any of His Majesty's Forces, shall be guilty of an offence and punished accordingly. Therefore the next issue of the "Chronicle" contained the following pernitent paragraph:

"The phrase had been used in wounded soldiers' letters, and may have contained some currency, that the 7th battalion had been cut up. Any such phrase should certainly not be accepted in its literal sense. Perhaps it was undesirable to use it at all; and I grieve to hear that in some instances it had unintentionally caused distress to those whom everyone would desire to spare added pain in a time of grave anxiety.This journal may itself have unwittingly offended in giving prominence to the phrase. If so, I am sure editor and staff alike are profoundly sorry: indeed, I will go further, and hope all concerned will accept an expression of sincere regret."

'One would be willing to accept this apology had it had been made in a full and frank manner without the subtle or untrue inference that other papers had sinned the same. The suggestion by the "Chronicle" that "perhaps" it "may" have offended when it knows only too well it has done so, makes it desirable that for the sake of the public as well as the reputation of journalism, there should be this salutary reminder that the incident cannot pass without public protest. And why should the Editor drag in his staff in his laboured expression of regret? Is it not one of the first elements of editorial etiquette to take responsibilities in such cases. But apparently one cannot judge the "Chronicle" by any normal standards, even in war time.'

Whilst this local feud was going on, the relatives of the men in the 7th had to wait for news. Edgar Mobbs carrying out his duties to the best of his ability, wrote to as many relatives as he could, telling them of their men who had been killed, wounded or missing. This must have been a painful duty for him, for many of these men had joined him at Franklin's Gardens. None of then, not even Edgar himself, could have ever imagined that they would become so embroiled with a war, that with its technical advances had become a nightmare.

Back at the front the 7th realised that they had lost 402 men, killed, wounded and missing. The only clear information to hand was in regard to officer casualties. Colonel Parking had been killed, Captain V.D.Short and Lieutenant L.L.Phipps had also lost their lives. Major J.W.Fisher, Captain T.G.Paget, Lieutenant A.O.Marshall, Second Lieutenant C.F.Saunders

THE MOBBS' OWN

were wounded. Captain D.Farrar slightly wounded and remained on duty. Lieutenants J.N.Morley and Urquhart were known to have been wounded and missing.

Lieutenant Colonel P.C.B.Skinner arrived and took over command from Major Compton on the 3rd October 1915. Colonel Skinner was a career officer. A slight man full of energy, his main task was to reorganise the battalion and restore its morale.

The following day, even though most of the men had lost their equipment, the battalion was inspected by Major General Capper C.B. the new commander of the 24th division and a noted fire eater. The general addressed the men and told them that they had done well, but could have done better, which he was certain they would do in the future.

Because of the losses of officers in the brigade and the 7th having been fortunate in officer casualties, the following officers were lent out to the 9th Royal Sussex: Second Lieutenants J.C.Gurney, Motion, Hadly and Meadway.

As these extracts have been taken from the battalion war diary, without a doubt, written under severe conditions,the information was often sketchy, such as the initials given to J.C.Gurney, but not to the others.

There was a supreme effort from the regimental depot to fill the gaps left in the 7th and on the 7th October 50 NCO's and men arrived, included 19 men who had been slightly wounded in the offensive and had been returned for duty. The 3rd Northamptons sent the following officers, all Second Lieutenants: H.G.F.Shepherd, G.B.Bodges, A.F.Burnham, C.F.D.Hathornson, and H.N.Williamson.

In Northampton the reality of the situation became apparent, by this time the relatives of the men had received notifications, the majority of them being missing believed killed.

Local papers had information to hand and wrote of the battalion's cemetery at Vermotelle. Perrier bottles were used to inscribe the rank name and number of the man killed, until such times as an appropriate memorial could be made. The 'Chronicle' mentioned that after Colonel Parkin had been killed, Captain Mobbs commanded the battalion until Major Compton took over. The paper went to great pains to advise its readers that Major Compton had no connection with the Marquess of Northampton although he bore their family name.

Some information was given about Colonel Skinner, who had been a brigadier with Botha in West Africa, and was accepted as a true soldier by the men of the 7th. The position of second in command was then given to Edgar Mobbs who played a great part in restoring the shattered morale of the battalion which had suffered such grevious losses.

Heavily censored letters did manage to come through from the men of the 7th battalion and these were published in the local papers. They are worthy of repeat because they give a simple soldier's version of what happened to the battalion at Loos.

> 'I shall never forget those terrible days of the great advance. It was my first real glimpse of warfare, and it will remain impressed in my mind as long as memory lasts. We marched for two days to our position, spending the night in the open, and on Saturday night took over our trenches. All the time a terrible cannonade was going on, deafening by day, but ten times more terrible at night, when the vivid flashes in the sky, like sustained summer lightning, the lingering lights of the star shells, as they burst, and the roar of the artillery seemed almost to herald the end of time and the approach of eternity.
>
> 'Sunday came, and the light of the day brought relief to our tense nerves, and we were glad to get the order to move, no matter the consequences, after the nerve wrecking noises of the night before.

THE MOBBS' OWN

When the order came along, we sprang from our trenches and dashed, yelling as we went, towards the Germans. It seemed as if ten thousand furies had been suddenly let loose. How we reached the German trenches I cannot recall. All I remember is hand-to-hand work with the bayonet until we secured the trench and dropped down on the soft bodies of the German dead.

'When I had time to collect my wits I looked eagerly around at my comrades. There seemed few missing faces, and I think we escaped lightly. We held on to our position with hardly a bite or a drink no food could reach us there for some time, but it got too hot, and we were driven out. But back we came and won it again with the bayonet. Again a horrible night of vivid nightmares with the dead and the dying all around.

'The worst of Monday was worse than what had gone on before. We held a trench in a dangerously exposed position, and before it was light, shells fell thick and fast. It looked if nothing could live in it, yet we hung on, and with the trenches blown in, in places, and badly damaged all along, the Prussian Guard came to the attack. They seemed to have pushed across on either side and came at us from both ends. One machine gun was put out of action and we had to retire.

'Just a handful failed to get away with us and we gave them up as lost. They were cut off, but they held out for some time and eventually got away. The enemy, apparently under the impression that the trenches were better manned. Just afterwards I felt that all the mules in creation had kicked me. At least that is what it felt like when I got hit; and thus ended my experience of actual warfare.'

THE MOBBS' OWN

There was no name attached to this letter, which was vivid in its description with an excellent use of language, obviously the work of an educated man, possibly one of Edgar Mobbs' gentleman privates.

The second letter certainly has a ring of authenticity, written in a charming, homely tone, with some information deleted by the censor. The letter was written by Lance Corporal A.C.Holden to his wife at Little Houghton:

> 'We have been in the trenches about four days, going in on Saturday and coming out on Tuesday, since when we have been a considerable distance behind the firing line.
>
> 'Talk about an inferno, it was just about what I imagined it to be. Will Hammond who was at Doctor Greens was wounded, also Arthur Osborne, your cousin. He was about ten yards from me when he got hit with a piece of shrapnel in the thigh. It was only a flesh wound, I think, as he was able to walk. Sergt Crick had his arm rather badly hurt, and that fellow who was in the same house as me at Inkerman, named Gordon is missing, as are Sergt Stock and Pte Jack Gillam. Our casualties have been rather heavy. The Colonel killed, the Major injured, another captain killed, Capt Guy Paget and his brother in law (Major Mansfield) wounded and several other officers injured. Talk about brave fellows. You ought to see them Scotties. They stroll about all over the place on the top of the trenches with bullets flying around, taking not a bit of notice. By the way Sid Symonds had been wounded, but not very seriously.'

At that time the only official casualty list issued to the town was made up from 2 known dead, 65 wounded, 2 gassed and a small amount of men listed as missing. These figures had no bearing on the actual casualties.

THE MOBBS' OWN

The men listed were as follows:

Killed: Pte.S.C.Forscutt, Pte.Robert Prior.

Wounded: Major E.L.Mansfield. Capt.T.Guy Paget. Lieut.J.N.Morley.

Sergt. Baxter, Sergt. Boyson, Sergt. R.Ward, Sergt. F.Smith. Sergt. C.Harrison. Sergt. Crick, Sergt. H.R.Dickins, Sergt. J.Stevens, Sergt. Pettit, Corpl. E.J.Seddon. Corpl. E.Buswell, Lance Corpl. R.Jameson.

The following Private soldiers were also listed as having been wounded:

F.Tarry, B.King, C.P.Philpot, W.Walker, E.Mason, J.Parrott, F.Stimpson, A.E.Cleaver, A.W.Osborn, T.Twist, H.Dunkley, R.Richardson, C.Stapleton, P.A.L.Spanton, C.Brunswick, E.Gordon, F.Pugh, W.Panter, S.Sibley, A.L.Sharman, J.Dodson, V.Barker, W.Flowers, S.A.Rimes, R.E.Gilbert, W.Denton, T.Allibone, J.Percival, F.Cowley, H.Foster, F.Kirby, G.Teeboon, W.Hill, G.Fellows, E.T.Wise, P.Robinson, F.D.Tarry, A.Broughton, H.Featherstone, F.Bird, V.W.F.Harris, W.Toomes, E.J.Smith, F.W.Jeyes, F.Watts, R.Cooper, C.Willis, T.Sismey, S.C.Forscutt, J.F.Bird.

Pte. A.J.Wright, Pte. B.O.W.Smith, Pte. S.Baxter and Pte. E.Amos, were reported as being gassed, the record does not show whether this was German gas or British gas. As part of the British master plan was to use chlorine gas in the attack, it was possibly the latter.

One of the Army Chaplains at the front, the Rev. Sydney Groves who had been the curate of St. Mary's Kensington, wrote to his father who resided in Northampton. This letter was published in the Chronicle and to some extent supports the list of wounded mentioned:

> 'Although I am in no way connected with the 7th Northamptons (excepting for the fact that I am a native of the town.) the tides of fortune have worked me up against them, and I am able to send a

THE MOBBS' OWN

little news as to their doings. The division to which I am attached made a great attack on Friday in conjunction with two divisions on our right and left.

'The brigade of which the 7th Northamptons form part was hurried up to assist us, and I am afraid they had a pretty rough time of it, too. I must say it was very hard luck on them after a long march and quite unprepared and unaccustomed to the trenches to be rushed into what will probably prove to be the fiercest battle of the war.

'Owing to the great rush of wounded at present, it may be some time before the parents and friends receive any definite news outside the most unsatisfactory field service post card and the equally alarming wire from the War Office. I am sending a list of a few fellows I saw at an advanced dressing station, and I should like their relatives to know that they were bright and cheerful, and I hope by now, going on well. In some cases I have written, but as I have been writing letters for my own men for three days and nights. I am getting a bit weary.

'I may say that I have been out here nearly five months, and have seen thousands of wounded, and I have never yet heard a grumble or complaint. They are all perfectly splendid, and the Northamptons are no exception to the rule. They have done their bit for a time, and they have done it well.'

The editor in closing this correspondence stated that Pte. E.A.Cleaver is the second son of Mr Alfred Cleaver of Colwyn Road and Wood Street, and Sgt. Walter Crick is the second son of the late W.D.Crick a partner in the firm of Messrs. Crick and Co., boot manufacturer of Northampton.

THE MOBBS' OWN

The reformed 7th, now reequipped and reorganized, made the following promotions: Capt.H.Grierson to command 'A' Coy, Lieut.H.King to command 'B' Coy, Lieut. A.H.Flynn to command 'C' Coy and Captain D.Farrar to command 'D' Coy.

Following orders from brigade, the battalion was to relieve the Durham Light Infantry who were in trenches around the village of St. Eldi. This was the usual procedure for an infantry battalion to take over from another and stay in the trenches for a tour of duty. This was always dangerous. The main difficulty was to get a battalion to move out and another one in, without noise and the inevitable bussling. Noise excited the enemy who were apt to mortar the trenches or bring in artillery fire. The British line returned the compliment on German relief movements.

Coming out of the line, the relieved battalion would commence a rest period. This consisted of rebuilding trench work further back from the front line and the battalions were still subject to artillery barrages.

The 8th Northamptons drafted in further Second Lieutenants to fill up the complement of the 7th, they were: W.W.Taylor, A.B.Cox, E.G.Passmore, S.C.Percival and M.A.S.Vaile. Mortar fire from the Germans was consistently damaging the trench work killing 3 men and wounding 5. Because of the moonlight nights no work could be undertaken outside of the trenches.

Working parties became the norm, trenches needed to be rebuilt and when the nights were moonless these parties could leave the trenches. Because of this constant work being completed by both sides, the men were apt to ignore German workers in the hope that the enemy would do the same. Officers had to patrol and give order that the enemy, clearly in sight, must be fired upon.

A classic example of this tolerance from the ranks, when the attitude live and let live was often the case, was not felt by a sniper in the 11th Middlesex, who was a crack shot. Noticing the red tabs of a German staff officer eyeing the British line

THE MOBBS' OWN

through his field glasses, this marksman decided to shoot this German officer through the head. The Germans in their anger shelled the 12th Middlesex for two days and that sniper was far from popular as many of his comrades were killed and wounded as a result.

Holding this section of the line between the 13th and 23rd October the Northamptons were relieved by the 13th Middlesex, who with the Royal Sussex made up their brigade. During these ten days of duty the 7th lost 5 men killed and 9 wounded.

The men of the battalion had little rest, there were kit inspections and cleaning apart from the working parties repairing trench work. There was a welcome addition of a further 100 men drafted in to make up some of the losses from the battle of Loos.

On the 27th October 20 lucky men were selected from the battalion to form part of a composite battalion that was to be inspected by the King at Reninghelst. These men were favoured because they all managed to get into a bath. These baths alloted to these men were the first the battalion had been allowed since arriving in France.

This inspection by the King had an historical significance. Sir John French's position as commander in chief of the BEF was now in some doubt, mainly due to the handling of his Army at Loos. His Majesty had a well earned reputation as being a dreadful horseman. French, in his wisdom ordered Sir Douglas Haig to find a mount for the King that was gentle in temperament and a pleasure to ride. In accordance with his instructions, Haig, already held in high esteem by the King, found a suitable mount.

The division lined up ready for the King's inspection. For reasons unknown the King's horse reared, the King fell off and the mount fell on him, creating heavy bruising which took a great deal of time to heal.

There could be no excuses this time. French was relieved of

79

THE MOBBS' OWN

his command and given the responsibility of home defence. In his place, Sir Douglas Haig assumed command of the British Army and held that post until the end of the war.

Back at the front, Edgar and the 7th found conditions to be muddy and wet in the rear camps. The men were finding it very difficult to dry their clothing and there was little comfort in their existence. Fatigue parties were being constantly called upon, very often under the direction of the Royal Engineers. Some good news did come through, the battalion as a whole could make use of the divisional baths. Back in their camp the men made pathways from bully beef tins and ashes. Every effort was made to make their lives more tolerable. The battalion dropped in to a routine of relieving other regiments in the line, and then pulling back to rest, continue their training and being involved in repairing trench works. During this period of routine, men were being killed and wounded, mainly through artillery fire. There was no time when a soldier could relax.

At Christmas the men enjoyed their puddings sent to them through a fund supported by the people of Northampton. Extra items were on offer in the canteen, such as cigars, oranges and beer. On the 28th December Lieutenants H.B.King and R.Gurney were promoted to the rank of Captain and continued to command their companies.

In the New Year Edgar was allowed home leave and the Northampton people eagerly awaited him in the hope that he could furnish them with some news about the men reported as missing from the 7th.

The only true authentic casualty list that had been published was in connection with the officers, the families of the other ranks were still, partially, kept in ignorance. Edgar explained that the delay was caused through men, who had lost contact with their units still coming in and reporting themselves as survivors. Furthermore many men had been taken prisoner and this had to be confirmed by the Germans, who were never in a great hurry to do this unless the Red

THE MOBBS' OWN

Cross intervened. Because of these reasons a casualty list could not be prepared or published.

This was true for as the late veteran Percy Slarke has said, his two best friends just vanished and that was still the case 50 years on. Presumed dead could be the only term to cover these men, and that in itself was unsatisfactory for their loved ones.

Rumour had been rife in Northampton about a forged signal that had ordered the 7th to pull out of their line during the early part of the battle. The only official mention of this was that some of the men did pull out and were ordered back by officers, there was no mention of this incident in the War Diary of the battalion. The local papers even used the term 'Spy' and stated that a German agent was responsible. The human aspect of this pull out should be considered. It would require an iron discipline to hold a line against fierce enemy action, if one or two men lost their nerve and left the line, they could easily be followed by others.

Edgar had to answer to this rumour neither denying or admitting to the question of a spy. With his usual spirit he defended the 7th Battalion, 'They stood their ground as Northampton men can.' Edgar refused to accept any criticism directed against his comrades. Once again the conditions of the long march to the field of battle was mentioned, their shortage of food and water, in fact it was a surprise that the 7th had done so well, seeing that it was their first baptism of fire. Their ordeal would have tried the nerves of seasoned soldiers, so it could be well realised what it meant to young men most of whom before the war were strangers to soldiering and pursuing peaceful callings in local business houses.

Mr.Holloway true to his constant participation in the war effort, requested that if relatives had heard that their men had been taken prisoner, then he should be advised, so that food parcels could be allocated.

Four

On his return to the battalion, Edgar discovered that Colonel Skinner was to take temporary command of the 73rd Infantry Brigade to allow Brigadier General Jelf to go on leave. As this left the 7th without a commanding officer, Edgar was promoted to a major and assumed command in the absence of Colonel Skinner. This was a remarkable promotion. In the peace time Army an officer would have to serve at least 15 years to obtain a field rank, Edgar had managed this in 15 months.

To prevent confusion over rank, the modern day Army does not have brigadier generals only brigadiers. In 1915 a brigadier general wore the badge of rank of crossed swords, a further star would make him a major general and if that star was replaced with a crown he would become a lieutenant general, a full general would have crossed swords a star and a crown to denote his rank. A brigadier in our modern Army wears three stars and a crown, the further senior ranks have not changed.

The battalion was constantly on the move to various sectors of the front, then resting in base camps. Edgar inspecting the huts of the men, put up a prize of 40 francs for the best kept hut and awarded this to 'A' company, showing in his own way that it was the 7th Battalion that mattered to him, not just his beloved 'D' company.

On the 13th January 1916, Lieutenant Colonel Skinner resumed his command of the 7th.

In the regimental diaries constant mention is made of the direction of the wind, being either dangerous or safe. This is connected with the enemy's use of poisonous gas. If the wind

THE MOBBS' OWN

was in the direction of the German lines it was safe, otherwise it could be dangerous.

In the trenches at Hooge the men found that conditions were appalling, and working parties were ordered to improve the fortifications and drainage. because of the closeness of the enemy this had to be done at a slow rate, using a few men, otherwise the Germans would shell the trenches, hoping to retard progress.

The men finishing this duty in the line were supplied with cocoa and soup by the division as they rested in the Ypres Asylum. By this time it was realised that due to the conditions in the trenches the men should be issued with gum boots (Wellingtons). Because of a shortage of this footwear the men had to hand them in as soon as they left the line so other incoming battalions could use them.

One of the most common conditions afflicting the battalion, apart from the ever presence of lice, was trench foot. If a man stood in either wet or damp conditions over a period of days, without being able to remove his boots, then a fungi would attack his feet, in many cases inflicting a crippling condition. In time the Army issued an ointment to treat this problem, which was difficult for the men in the trenches to use, because it was rare when they were in a position to remove footwear. What they did find was that it had an inflammable nature, that assisted them in lighting fires for their brew up.

Life in the battalion was devoted to tours of duty in the trenches followed by rest periods of a doubtful nature. There were always church parades on Sundays and various training schemes being organised apart from working parties repairing trench works. Men were trained as specialists, this would comprise signallers, Lewis gun crews and Mortar squads.

The 7th were selected to experiment and try out mats, designed to lay over barbed wire, to allow platoons to cross over these obstacles, which could impede any frontal assault. Lieutenant Goode supervised these exercises and as a result of his report the mats were issued to the 9th Royal Sussex.

On the 13th February 1916 the 7th relieved the 2nd Battalion the Leinster Regiment, an Irish regiment with which the 7th would have a close, operational connection in the near future. The Leinsters was just one of the Irish regiments that served with such distinction in the British Army.

During this tour of duty the battalion lost its intelligence officer, Second Lieutenant I.H.Stevenson. This officer went over the top one night to examine the barbed wire along the battalion's lines. The Germans seeing him, opened fire, with rifles, bombs and trench mortars. Colonel Skinner ordered a patrol to go and bring this officer back. No trace could be found and it was assumed that he had been killed.

For the first time the Army was issued with steel helmets to replace the soft service cap, which offered no protection to its wearer. These helmets were called " shrapnel proof," and did offer some chance of escaping head injuries, but to say they were shrapnel proof was an overstatement.

On the 29th February, Lieutenant Colonel Skinner once again assumed command of the 73rd brigade, leaving Edgar Mobbs to command the 7th.

The weather now became severe, making trench life close to intolerable. Heavy snow fell and a new enemy struck the battalion, frost bite.

News came through that acting Brigadier General Skinner had been admitted to hospital as a sick man. The brigade was then commanded by Lieutenant Colonel Bullen Smith the commanding officer of the Leinsters. No replacement was sent to the 7th and Edgar Mobbs still assumed command.

The regimental diaries at this stage record incidents that are mainly repetitive. Men were still being killed and wounded on a regular basis, mainly by what the diary calls: whiz bangs and crumps, the crumps denoting heavy artillery and the whiz bangs mainly mortar fire, both names describing the noise these weapons made on detonation.

THE MOBBS' OWN

Coming into the welcome warmth of Spring, Edgar was promoted to the rank of Lieutenant Colonel after commanding the battalion with distinction. This was not a selection approved with ease. The general staff did object to temporary officers, serving for the length of hostilities, being given promotion to command battalions. There were still plenty of regular officers who could have filled this vacancy. With the 7th battalion was an uniqueness, that being Edgar Mobbs. The 7th battalion was Edgar Mobbs, one could not be seperated from the other, and it was natural that Edgar's position should be confirmed with this promotion.

For the month of May the battalion lost 1 officer wounded, 3 other ranks killed and 24 wounded. With these figures it could be calculated that a battalion could loose over 300 men a year, by merely carrying out trench duties, without being involved in a major offensive. There was still a crying need for replacements to fill the gaps left by these men.

Once Edgar had taken command of his men in a regular and confirmed capacity, he insisted that they should be recognised for their individual gallantry. As a consequence, the following men were decorated: Lieutenant P.S.Hadley was awarded the Military Cross. Sergeant A.M.Ruston, Corporal J.T.Jackson, Corporal R.Twentyman and Lance Corporal C.Fitch were awarded the Military Medal. Sergeant A.E.Allebone was awarded the Distinguished Conduct Medal.

Decorations were allocated to divisions, and relied upon recommendations from commanding officers. Military Crosses always out numbered Military Medals, because of anticipated qualities of leadership accruing from the officers and was also a reflection upon officer losses. It was due to the insistence of Edgar Mobbs that these decorations came to the 7th.

On the 16th of June Edgar had a welcome addition to his nominal roll, in the shape of Major Dobbin who was a regular officer from the 1st battalion. It was evident that even a man of Edgar's calibre would struggle with the day to day

85

THE MOBBS' OWN

administration of a battalion, the nuances of military compliance could not be mastered in a matter of months.

The day after the arrival of Major Dobbin, the enemy attacked the brigade's lines with gas. The 9th Royal Sussex facing the largest release of gas which actually entered their headquarter's area. Previous to this attack the Germans had swept the line with heavy machine gun fire and by doing so gave a clear indication that they were going to use gas. The course of action was intended to prevent the brigade from a clear observation and not be aware of the wind bringing over the gas. As it happened the men were wearing their respirators apart from 10 men of the 7th, who suffered gas poisoning. The Germans followed this up with a heavy artillery barrage upon the brigade front. Normally this would herald an attack by infantry. As the British were aware of this they answered with their own barrage which prevented the enemy infantry from leaving their trenches.

As a result of this action the 7th lost 33 men. In time the bombardment fell away and the men were required to wear their gas helmets for a further one hour and a half. The final result of the action resulting in the battalion losing 1 officer wounded, 7 other ranks killed and 53 wounded.

Because of the effectiveness of the gas helmets and the brigade, mainly negating the gas attack, 200 of the men involved went to Dranoutre to be inspected by General Plumer who commanded the 2nd Army. It had long been considered that the character of Colonel Blimp was based upon this General. This man's portly presence, round, red face, belied his ability as the finest Army commander in the war.

Whilst relieving the 2nd Leinsters, enemy artillery bombarded the lines and the 7th loss 30 men, including Second Lieutenant A.F.J.Burnham. It would have been a sad and trying time for Edgar Mobbs who could only watch men from his battalion being wasted away. During the month of June the 7th had lost 1 officer and 11 other ranks killed and 101 wounded.

THE MOBBS' OWN

The time had now come for the 7th battalion to be engaged in a major battle, the battle of the Somme. Edgar had received his orders from brigade and quickly studied the part his battalion would take in this new offensive.

For the first time the 7th would go into a major action under the command of Edgar Mobbs and this time they were all confident that they would better their performance at Loos.

Because of the French Army holding out at Verdun, their influence upon the Western Front was diminished and the part of the line occupied by the French for the assault only amounted to eight miles, their divisional strength fell from 40 divisions to 16, and in the actual offensive only 5 divisions took part. This left the British Army to take on the main burden and this was mainly the case during the rest of the war. In the battle of the Somme the British occupied the line from Ypres to the Somme a total of eighty miles.

Haig had devised a master plan, his main object being to over run the German lines. This was to be proceeded by a continuous heavy artillery bombardment. Because of the artillery zeroing their range, the 7th did have British shells landing on the lip of their own trenches. It was during these early hours of the attack that Edgar was hit by shrapnel. The trajectory of shrapnel is a matter of fate. The shell itself can disperse tiny fragments of shrapnel or large pieces as big as bricks. If the shrapnel hits a man with its cutting edge it causes horrendous wounds,if the trajectory is flat, then the shrapnel will hit a man at a tremendous velocity without cutting the victim. It was a flat sedgement of shrapnel that hit Edgar Mobbs in his ribs. In much agony, badly bruised and winded he insisted upon carrying on. The task was impossible, no man can lead a battalion into an assault when he himself can hardly walk. Edgar was taken to a base hospital at the rear and was compelled to leave his battalion.

An experienced officer was quickly drafted in from the Leinsters in the shape of Major Paddy Murphy M.C. This dark and handsome Irishman was well liked by the men of the

THE MOBBS' OWN

battalion and they had every confidence in his ability to lead them into the attack.

The men waited for the officer's whistles to tell them to get over the top and advance. Once again it was the question of weight. Each man had to carry 66 lbs, over half his own body weight. This made it impossible for them to advance any quicker than a slow walk, there could never be an heroic charge. Because of their numbers the men would bunch. One of the most difficult tasks for an infantry officer is to get his men spaced out, it is all part of the human communion for men to stay close and as a result presenting a larger target to the enemy.

Percy Slarke now a sergeant, experienced a bee like noise as hundreds of particles hit his face and blinded him (happily, Percy recovered his sight), even 50 years later, he would find particles of shrapnel on his pillow, minute pieces of shell that had left his flesh during the night.

The 7th made slow advance finding the German resistance heavy and bogging them down in open country with very little cover apart from shell holes, normally filled with water.

The 9th Royal Sussex were on the left flank of the 7th and the 13th Middlesex on their right. It was important for a battalion's flanks to be protected otherwise the enemy can work their way round and attack from the rear. Paddy Murphy realised that his right flank was open, the 7th were dangerously exposed. The l3th Middlesex had a set task in the attack. They were to occupy a village station, guarded by two German machine gun emplacements. Sending out a runner, Paddy Murphy wanted to know what had happened to the 13th Middlesex, were they hemmed down and would follow up later, or were they still held in their trenches? The runner came across 33 men commanded by a full corporal. They were the sole survivors of the 13th Middlesex which had been wiped out by the two German machine guns, all their officers had died and the rest of the battalion were either killed or wounded they had been annihilated! The 7th had to spread

THE MOBBS' OWN

their line out making up the ground which should have been occupied by the 13th Middlesex.

The story of this battalion was very close to what happened to the British Army. The men had to wait for 48 hours before they went into the attack, and during that time the trenches were flooded with rain and the heavy artillery denied them sleep. The weather was hot and sticky. The Germans waited for the barrage to subside then returned to their machine guns and waited for the waves of British infantry.The battalions attacked in 4 or 8 waves, never more than a 100 yards separated them, an easy target for German machine guns. By nightfall the Army had lost thousands of their men, many of the battalions which should have been over seven hundred in strength had less than a hundred men. That single day's losses were the heaviest the Army was to suffer, and the Army was mainly made up from the Kitchener battalions of 1914/15.

On the 20th August Paddy Murphy returned to his regiment and Captain N.B.King commanded the survivors of the 7th.

The initial figures recorded in the war diary were as follows:

5 Officers killed, 45 other ranks killed. 15 officers wounded, 258 other ranks wounded. 1 officer missing and 49 other ranks.

A list of officer casualties were recorded, but not other ranks:

Killed: Second Lieutenants G.V.Knott, H.Lloyd, N.S.Ball, A.C.D.Page, and M.B.Lea.

Wounded: Lieutenant Colonel E.R.Mobbs. Captain H.Grierson. Lieutenants A.B.Cox. S.H.Motion,P.S.Hadley, R.T.B.Houghton. Second Lieutenants E.G.Butcher, H.Harris, C.D.Morgan, E.H.Morris, A.W.Holland, N.Mattock, A.Durrant Swan, C.A.Debenham and C.F.Saunders.

Like the rest of the Army the 7th did not fulfil their actual target, but conducted themselves well in the face of heavy resistance. A letter was received from Paddy Murphy who complimented the battalion on their conduct under fire.

Major E.Lascelles of the 11th Rifle Brigade arrived to assume command of the battalion in the continued absence of Edgar Mobbs.

During August the battalion occupied the front at Fricourt and due to a heavy bombardment lost 5 killed and 25 wounded.

Major Lascelles returned to his regiment and Major T.H.S. Swanton of the East Surrey Regiment assumed command.

Paddy Murphy did not allow the absence of Edgar Mobbs to undermine the morale of the battalion, as a result of recommendations following the offensive, the following awards were granted in September:

Corporal Bunyan, Privates J.Blake, S.Childs, K.E.Barby, F.Warley, E.Carr and W.West were all awarded the Military Medal.

Back at home the news of the offensive and the regiment's losses was once again fragmentary. The Independent published the limited news that had come through:

> 'Although no details have yet been published concerning the recent engagement on the Somme in which the 7th Battalion took a gallant part, the casualty lists bear witness to the heavy price that had been paid by the corps. All officers, including Colonel Mobbs, were wounded but a few of them escaped with such minor injuries that they were able to remain with the remnants of the Regiment. The Battalion succeeded in taking a most important position held by the enemy and retained it most gallantly in the face of a very severe bombardment. The brave tenacity with which the 7th held on against a positive inferno of shot and shell forms one of the most thrilling and heroic episodes of the war. The splended stand of the 7th soon became known along the line and when they returned to

THE MOBBS' OWN

camp on relief they were greeted with rousing cheers. It is a pity the veil cannot be more fully lifted on the heroic deeds of our County Battalions for they have dared and done as much as any of those more fortunate to enjoy the limelight of national fame and public eulogy.'

By the 23rd of September many of the men wounded at the Somme were returning. As Percy Slarke had indicated, the base hospitals soon returned them to duty. If your wound was not a Blighty wound, back to the front you went.

The question of men being released from hospitals both in France and England was a contentious issue. Because of heavy losses in areas, men were not sent back to their own units as a matter of course, they were used to fill up holes in other battalions. This was a certainty to reduce morale and was a short sighted policy, failing to take into consideration regimental pride and the loss of friends.

One activity that was always with the 7th was the need to send out fighting patrols over towards the enemy lines. A fighting patrol was made up of 1 officer, 7 scouts, 4 bombers, 3 Lewis gunners and 1 runner. The aims of these patrols, were to attack enemy patrols, take prisoners, obtain information, destroy a troublesome enemy machine gun or obtain equipment for intelligence purposes.

In October, a fighting patrol of the Leinsters captured a prisoner, whilst being on the flanks of the 7th. The next morning a fighting patrol of the 7th was engaged by an alert enemy with a result that its leader Lieutenant C.L.Clarke was killed. That same night Second Lieutenant R.E.Duchesne was killed whilst inspecting the Battalion's wire.

The following morning a fighting patrol under the command of Lieutenant Shankster, accompanied by Second Lieutenant B.Wright, no doubt included to gain experience, raided the enemy line and inflicted casualties. In the fighting Lieutenant Shankster was shot dead, and Second Lieutenant

THE MOBBS' OWN

Wright was shot in the leg but managed to bring the patrol back to the battalion's lines.

In that tour of duty which had lasted 9 days, the Battalion lost 3 officers and 4 other ranks killed, and 16 men wounded including 1 officer.

On the 25th October the Battalion welcomed back their Colonel. Edgar Mobbs had made sufficient recovery to return to his command.

It was during this period that a young Second Lieutenant was made Battalion intelligence officer. This young man was slight and dimunitive and wore glasses. His name was Berridge. By the end of the war this officer had reached the rank of captain and had been awarded no less than 3 Military Crosses and was awarded the Distinguished Service Order in the Victory Honours. Research has discovered that this officer had actually been recommended for the Victoria Cross, this recommendation was not approved and in its place he was awarded his 3rd Military Cross. Colonel Berridge was not aware of this, the recommendation having been held in the private papers of the former orderly room sergeant of the battalion. He was informed when he was over eighty years of age. It is worthy of record to state, that this officer was the most highly decorated man in the 7th Battalion.

The officer and men who had been awarded decorations had them presented by General Plumer, Edgar Mobbs and two hundred selected men from the 7th were on parade to see their comrades being honoured.

It was a sign that Edgar Mobbs had returned, for the Battalion managed to play a soccer match against the Sherwood Foresters and beat them 2 - 1.

In December the Battalion lost Captain Gurney who had been one of the original Mobbs' Corps as he was to join the 72nd Infantry brigade to be trained as a Staff Captain. It is of interest to note that Captain Gurney was the son of the Vicar of St. Giles Church, Northampton.

It was during December of that year that Edgar Mobbs became a sick man because of his previous chest wound. This wound had affected his respiratory system and as a result he suffered from bouts of bronchitis and added to this he was plagued with trench foot. This once, fine athlete, was confined to his bed with a high fever. The responsibilities of command and life in the trenches were taking their toll and a great deal of concern was registered throughout his Battalion.

The 7th was being rebuilt. On the 13 December 113 men were drafted to the Battalion, 11 of them being veterans returning to active service after being wounded in the 7th and a further 27 men having served in other regiments at the front. The remainder had no experience of active service and Edgar Mobbs ordered them back to training camps.

Every effort was made to make the men of the battalion more comfortable whilst in base camp. At Les Brebis 'C' and 'D' companies had refreshment and entertainment organised by the Reverend E.U.Evitt.

Since Haig had taken command of the British Army, every major action that was undertaken was plagued with heavy rain, in fact it was close to an every day occurrence. The 7th suffered in this way, the trenches fell into an awful condition, the rain flooding the lines and in places became three feet deep. This only added to the dehumanizing effect that the soldier suffered. Veterans have stated that human life was devalued by these conditions. The walls of damaged trench work, softened by the constant rain, would reveal human debris, arms and legs of French soldiers that had once defended these lines. It was not uncommon to use skulls of dead soldiers as candle holders. Then there was the smell, a putrification that would remain with these men all their lives, the unique odour of the dead, wafting in from no man's land, where the corpses could never be recovered. The Army did not recognise the modern term: battle fatigue, the men who lost both their mental and physical control were labelled as shell shocked.

On the 3rd January 1917 news came through that Edgar Mobbs had been awarded the Distinguished Service Order. As the name of this decoration implies it is not awarded for once single act of gallantry, constant service of a distinguished nature results in the recipient being so honoured. To command a battalion on active service, with distinction was the reason for Edgar being recommended for this award.

The raids on the trenches continued. In late January during heavy frost the Germans raided the lines held by the 7th and mainly directed towards 'D' company. This enemy party attacked at 3 oclock in the morning, after a heavy bombardment. The Germans entered the trenches and fighting commenced between the men of 'D' company and the eighty members of the raiding party. 'D' company drove the enemy out of their trenches killing the German officer commanding and 5 others. One member of 'D' company being wounded was dragged away by the Germans. On approaching the enemy wire, this man managed to escape and returned to his own line. Heavy mobile charges had been left by the enemy near the Battalions wire, and patrols were sent out to clear them.

On the 8th February 1917 Edgar was granted his first local leave from the front, which was normally taken in Paris and Major Millard assumed command. Before leaving Edgar had organised the battalion's soccer team to participate in the brigade's championship. Their first match was against the 73rd Machine Gun Company and the 7th won 5-0. A few days later they played against the Light Trench Mortar Battery and beat them 11-0. There was still a strong element of sportsmen within the battalion. Entering the semifinal round they were matched against the 9th Royal Sussex and beat them 12-2. Arriving at the finals the team to beat was the 73rd Brigade Headquarters and once again it was a resounding victory winning by a margin of 4-1. General J.E. Capper the divisional commander presented the team with a silver cup.

THE MOBBS' OWN

During the month of March, the battalion's casualties were light, being 7 men killed and 20 wounded. The weather had been severe, both sides suffering from freezing fog.

The next tour of duty involved far greater movement than the men had become accustomed to.

The Allied high command had been planning a major offensive for some time and because there was little agreement between the French and the British, coupled with the fact that the French Army was suffering with a low morale and many of their divisions could not be relied upon, this offensive did not take place until the summer of 1917.

The German high command in March 1917, either through their intelligence reports or through tactical reasons, reduced their holdings on the Somme and pulled back. Haig, feared that the Germans might be switching their troops north to attack his Army in Flanders.

Haig's fear was unfounded, the German commander Ludendorff was pulling back to a new defensive position which the Germans named as the Siegfried Line, not to be accused of a lack of imagination the allies called this, the Hindenburg Line.

Edgar Mobbs was now back from his leave and his battalion was soon involved with this German reorganisation of their line.

The weather was very poor with heavy snow in this early April of 1917. The British artillery was involved in heavy shelling targeting Vimy Ridge and the German lines at Bois En Hache. As was the general rule, shells did drop short and many hit the trench lips and killed Private Hines. This soldier was Edgar Mobbs' runner and as such could not have been far away from his Colonel at the time of his death.

The strategy of the high command was to carry a limited assault upon the area of Vimy ridge. The plan being to draw in the German reserves and by doing so, weaken them and make them less effective during the forthcoming major

95

assault. Haig was aware that the German manpower situation was just as critical as that suffered by the allies, at this stage of the war the German army was outnumbered.

To shake German morale the British had been mining the Vimy ridge area for some considerable time, without the enemy detecting this operation. Vast quantities of explosives were stacked into this area and just prior to the offensive detonated. Cutlery on tables in London, moved with the shock waves of this explosion. This was followed by intense and prolonged artillery fire. What Haig's staff had not realised was that it was mainly farmland they were shelling, with the consequence that drainage was destroyed by the artillery. The rain did arrive, as always when Haig carried out a major offensive. The battle area became a sea of mud, and in these dreadful conditions the infantry had to struggle through and attempt to fight. Many of the men wounded, fell and drowned in these close to flood conditions.

On the 7th April it was ordered that the Leinsters and the 9th Royal Sussex should attack the enemy lines at Bois En Hache, the 7th Northamptons were to be held back in support. During this attack the Canadian division was to attack Vimy Ridge.

Sir Douglas Haig always used his colonial troops as spearheads. It was true that these tough, uncomprising Canadians were excellent fighters, not subjected to the rigid class distinctions that pervaded the British Army.

The 9th April saw the British artillery continuing their shelling in Vimy Ridge allowing the Canadians to attack the Ridge south of the Pimple. The Leinsters fully prepared to attack the German lines had their orders cancelled. This was not to last for long, for on the 13th April the Irishmen went into their attack, and as a consequence suffered heavy losses together with the 9th Royal Sussex. The 7th were ordered to attack that night on a front of 200 yards and in their turn the order was cancelled and they were ordered to stand to.

It was at this period that the Germans exercised an orderly

THE MOBBS' OWN

and planned retreat. The 7th did leave their trenches and found they could advance over the empty German lines without losses, which must have been a welcome relief to Edgar Mobbs, who must have been fearing for his battalion.

It was an incredible fact that the 13th Middlesex were active on this front, the entire battalion having been replaced in a short time. The British Army did not allow regiments or their battalions to become defunct through losses.

A major disaster came very close to the 7th. This was not directly caused by the enemy but by their own commanders. Because of the unhindered advance of the brigade, the General Officer Commanding, together with the Brigadier General Commanding accompanied by the Brigade Major decided to inspect the lines. Unarmed, they were walking down the line at Bois de Riaumont when they were confronted by three Germans brandishing revolvers. These officers made a hasty exit, which no doubt would have been the talk of the division. Furious at this intrusion Major General Capper ordered an immediate search by the 7th. Two platoons carried out searches through the adjoining woods but failed to find the enemy.

House to house fighting was a new experience for Edgar Mobbs and his men. This came about by the Germans using houses for their sniper fire. Because of this, Edgar ordered Second Lieutenants Berridge and Morris to take a party and occupy all the houses stretching down the road from Lens to Bois de Riaumont. These officers managed to occupy the houses with little resistance from the enemy.

During this period of advance the battalion lost 61 men 17 of whom were killed.

For a few days the battalion was rested, if being involved in constant fatigues could be called resting.

On the 1st June during very hot weather the 7th arrived at Swan Chateau and worked on their own dugouts. Occupying this area and constantly building trench works, they were attacked by artillery on the 7th of that month. This was not normal shelling as the Germans were using gas shells, causing a few casualties and making life very difficult for the battalion. During this persistant shelling which had now reverted to high explosives, Edgar was hit over his heart by flat shrapnel and was badly bruised. After some rest he insisted upon carrying on. This was the second time that he had been struck in such a manner. .

On the 10th June, Edgar leading his battalion on a further relief, was briefing his company commanders before entering the front line. A shell exploded close to them, the blast knocking them off their feet and covering them with debris. In time they recovered and attempted to overcome the shock they would have been suffering. Their Colonel was found to be unsteady and a wound was discovered in his neck which was now profusely bleeding. They, as company commanders insisted upon carrying on and gave orders that Edgar should receive attention.

Captain A.J.W.Cunningham of the Royal Army Medical Corps treated the wound and although Edgar was badly shaken and weakened through loss of blood, he continued to command his battalion.

During this period of advance across mainly deserted territory, the 7th were heavily shelled and as a result casualties amounted to 7 other ranks killed and 42 wounded.

Leaving the line and returning to a base camp, it was wisely decided that Edgar Mobbs should be rested. With his right arm in a sling to prevent pressure on his lacerated neck muscles he was allowed to have leave, and this was to be Blighty leave.

Many friends and acquaintances welcomed Edgar's return. They found that he was no longer the energetic, boisterous character that they had all loved. This time he was more circumspect, developing the philosophy of a soldier that did not expect to survive the war. Talking to one of his close personal friends he commented that he would never be home

THE MOBBS' OWN

again and this was the last time. The one attribute that Edgar wanted to be remembered by, was that he had done his best.

This inner feeling was not uncommon, soldiers seeing their friends killed day after day accepted the fact that it could happen to them. In Edgar's case there must have been a much stronger realisation. He had, through his own efforts taken many young men to France and many of them had died, and by doing so had been sacrificed to the war. If Edgar was the instigator, the driving force behind their volunteering, in justice how could he survive that terrible conflict? He had been wounded three times and still managed to pull through, the most frustrating element being, that each wound lost him the command of the 7th.

> One again 'Jupiter' of the Independent, which I am sure was in reality, the pen of W.H. Holloway was in full flow: 'The familiar form of Lt.Colonel Edgar Mobbs is again in our midst and although he was badly wounded and still wears his right arm in a sling, he may be numbered among the lucky ones, considering how many of his brother officers were laid low by the inferno of shot and shell he also faced so bravely. A message of congratulations and good wishes has been sent to the gallant Colonel by the Mayor on behalf of the town, and by the desire of the War Bazaar committee he has been invited to open the bazaar on one of the three days, but he is not certain as yet whether he will be at home until then. All those who have supported our soldier's Comfort Fund will be gratified to know that Colonel Mobbs has personally assured me that thanks to our fund no battalions at the front have been so well supplied with smokes and other comforts as the Northamptons. He says our gifts were appreciated more than he can express, especially the smokes, which reached them in places in the front line where it was impossible to buy any."They are a great

boom," he added, "and make the men forget the dangers and discomfort of life in the trenches."

'Those who have seen the wonderful film of the Battle of the Somme at the Temperance Hall this week will readily realise the truth of the Colonel's words, for in these pictures of the actual fighting we see the brave hearted and mud covered boys returning from the trenches fagged out but happy with their fags. At the dressing stations too one notices that the first thing the orderlies do is to pop cigarettes in the mouths of the wounded heroes, even before they attend their wounds. Captain Danby Cogan, who is still busy attending the wounded at the front, had also assured me that the cigarette works wonders in the spirit of the wounded men and our readers will be pleased to know that supplies are sent regularly from the 'Independents' Fund for Captain Cogan to distribute among his patients. What a pleasure it is to be able to cheer up the hearts of our heroes with these gifts will be realised with a deeper pleasure by those who have witnessed the war film. To see how light heartedly our gallant sons do and dare so much for our sake fills one with a greater love and sympathy mingled with the feeling that they deserve all and more than we can ever do for them in return.'

Readers who are keen supporters of the anti-smoking campaign will, no doubt, find this article horrendous. What should be born in mind that prior to the war the male working masses were apt to smoke pipes. Life in the trenches did not permit the leisurely contemplative life of a pipe smoker, so the habit of cigarette smoking was born on a mass scale.

There was to be little rest for Edgar, he returned to his command on the 25th June 1917 to find that his battalion had lost a further 6 officers one of them being killed, within the ranks 26 men had lost their lives and a further 90 sustained wounds. On the 2nd of July Major D.W.Powell joined the battalion. Powell was a regular officer and had, no doubt been posted to the 7th because of Edgar's injuries and poor state of health.

Warfare was now becoming more scientific. Battalions were preparing for forthcoming offences by studying ground and making models of areas which they would attack. Gone were the days of simply going over the top to engage an enemy of unknown firing power and crossing terrain they had little knowledge of. It was true that Haig, feeling that his armies were bogged down in trenches commenced a policy of attrition. He felt that it was impossible for his men to sweep through the trench work of the enemy, without wiping out his Army. The French command had already informed the British commander in chief that their army in the field was France's last gasp. There could be no replacements, there were no men left of suitable military age. This was true, for at the end of the war, one in three Frenchmen between the age of 18 and 45, were either killed, wounded or taken prisoner. The situation was so severe, that after the war the loss of manpower was so great, that the French Goverment made the use of contraceptives illegal. They needed a future generation of males.

This policy of attrition was a simple theory. Haig considered that if his Army was bogged down in a giant quagmire, then they must make constant contact with the enemy and kill them. Haig himself had intimated that if at the end the British losses were 1 million and the Germans had lost 1 million and a quarter, then we had won the war. To him it was the only way. Haig had ambitions to replace the British Government with a military command, feeling that the entire nation should be placed on a military war footing, pushing to one side, the prying and the criticism levelled at him by politicians who, in the main , were mere civilians. Lloyd

THE MOBBS' OWN

George blocked the Army which had been trained in England from going to France. His one fear being that Haig would have them slaughtered.

It was during this policy of attrition that Edgar prepared his command for a major assault. They played company soccer matches with men from the 1st North Staffords, this was calculated to build an entente between the men they would be with in the attack.

A course was denoted by flags in area and depth and the 7th together with the Leinsters carried out a mock attack. Everything was done to prepare the men, this time allowing each man in the ranks to know exactly what was expected from them, which was certainly a new innovation, mainly cultivated by the Canadian troops.

Once again the two battalions rehearsed their attacks and this time, British aircraft added to the panorama, mainly due to the presence of Field Marshall Sir Douglas Haig.

Everything was now ready, and as usual with the 7th the first step was to march 15 miles. Edgar insisted that the packs should be carried by transport, and as a result not one man fell out from the march. The next day, this time wearing their packs and steel helmets the battalion covered a further 4 miles. The weather was now very hot.

Edgar was delighted that next to them in their camp was the 6th Service Battalion The Northamptonshire Regiment. The men loosing no time played the 6th at football and cricket. They then moved on, with further route marches.

On the 28th July 1917 the battalion received its orders for the attack. On the 29th of that month the battalion moved into the front line and on the 31st 'A' and 'C' companies attacked the enemy lines at Shrewsbury Forest at 3-50 a.m.

At first the attack went well the 7th covering a reasonable amount of ground, even though resistance from the enemy was severe. It was reported to Edgar that the company on his right was being held down by German machine gun fire and

THE MOBBS' OWN

finding it difficult to cover the flanks of the advancing company.

It is not difficult to imagine what went through Edgar Mobbs' mind the 13th Middlesex, was the same tragedy going to happen to the 7th Northamptons? If this company was wiped out then a further company would have to continue the attack with the same dreadful result.

Ordering a detachment of men and Second Lieutenant Berridge to accompany him, Edgar collected hand grenades and prepared himself to attack the German Machine gun posts that were raking fire into his men. The other officers realising with horror what their Colonel was about to do, begged him to stop and stay in his command. For a battalion to loose its commanding officer when it was carrying out a major attack, would mean a loss of command. One could say that for a commanding officer to purposely expose himself to danger was an irresponsible act.

Edgar refused to listen to them, he was going forward, he refused to delegate this attack to another officer. The danger was obvious, as it was the company was hemmed down and found, because of the intense fire they could not move forward.

Moving forward over the open ground Edgar approached the enemy. Second Lieutenant Berridge, an officer with undoubted and proven courage, stuck by his Colonel and screamed out: 'For God's sake, sir, get down!' The huge figure did not get down. Ignoring the fire Edgar hurried forward seeking to get within a throwing range so that he could destroy the enemy emplacement with hand grenades. It was all in vain, the German crew picked him up and fired into him and Egar fell, mortally wounded.

> The regimental diary recorded this tragic incident in soldiers' words: 'The battalion's 'A' and 'C' companies attacked the enemy line at Shrewsbury Forest at 3.50 a.m. this morning, during which the

commanding officer Lieut Colonel E.R.Mobbs, D.S.O. was killed.'

There is an excellent report, which although unsigned was no doubt written by Major Powell. It is included in its entirety as it is felt that the loss of Edgar Mobbs and the action carried out by the 7th should be told in the words composed by a fellow officer.

'29th July 1917. Battalion H.Q. 'C', 'D' and 'B' companies went up the forward area in the afternoon and evening of the 29th July 1917. 'A' company were ordered to remain in camp on account of the trenches it was to occupy being flooded.

'A' company relieved part of the 9th Royal Sussex Regt in 5 front line posts and the trenches about IMAGE TRENCH.

'D' company took Canada Street Tunnels.

'B' company in LARCH WOOD TUNNELS.

'B' company suffered 5 other ranks casualties through gas shells on the march to the forward area and Lieut Cawston was wounded. The other companies had no casualties.

'Owing to the heavy rain and many shell holes the ground was in a very bad condition.

'Battalion headquarters was established in Canada Street Tunnels which were very wet and crowded with troops, making progress through the tunnel very slow.

'30th July 1917. Situation normal throughout the day except that the enemy artillery heavily shelled IMAGE SUPPORT, ILLUSIVE SUPPORT and CENTRAL AVENUE at 1.45 a.m. and 4.00 p.m. Enemy split red lights preceeding the formal shelling.

'A' company marched from camp and occupied METROPOLITAN and left at 4.00 p.m. where they rested and had tea at night time.

A conference of company commanders was held at Battalion H.Q. at 5.00 p.m. and notification that zero hour for the attack on the following morning was to be at 3.50 a.m.was received before the conclusion of the meeting. Correct time for synchronization.

'About 9.30 p.m. Lt.Colonel Mobbs D.S.O. went with Lt.Colonel Murphy D.S.O. M.C. the O.C. of the 2nd Leinster Regiment and 2nd Lt.F.R.Berridge M.C. (intelligence officer 73rd Infantry Brigade) to ascertain the position of the stakes, which had been previously put out by the 9th Royal Sussex, to mark the out flanks of the assaulting Companies of the two battalions in their forming up positions. These were found by moonlight and 2nd Lt.Berridge remained out to put out the tape mark with which the companies would form up.

'31st July 1917. During the time Battalion headquarters were moved to another party of Canada Street Tunnels. 'A' and 'C' companies with 'D' company in support were formed up behind the tape line by 3.30 a.m. This operation was begun at midnight as it was necessary to allow plenty of time for the Companies to find their position without noise, and also for 'D' Company to get out of Canada Street Tunnels. Previous to zero (3.50 a.m.). The Germans were shelling moderately in No Mans Land causing some casualties among our troops who were forming up in attack. A general barrage fell 50 to 100 yards in front of our forming up line less than 3 minutes after zero causing rather heavy casualties, including 1 or 2 officers. At the same time enemy shells fell 100 to 150 yards behind our front line, but this could not be described as a barrage. The rapidity with which the enemy

105

barrage opened would appear to show that he was expecting the attack.

'Owing to darkness the assaulting companies were unable to keep a correct line, and also the men were inclined to bunch which is difficult to prevent until daylight. However owing to the same cause i.e. darkness, direction was undoubtedly lost from the beginning of the advance.

'It appears that the enemy machine guns were brought forward from JEER TRENCH into shell holes in front, before our barrage could reach them. They were thus quiet while our barrage was piling up on JEER TRENCH.

'Our assaulting troops being held up was unable to keep up with the barrage, lost direction, and became disorganized. The machine guns already referred to were dealt with, enabling a further advance to me made across JEER TRENCH, but once again German machine guns enfiladed us from the LOWER STAR post, which was then on our left flank and to our rear which the enemy still continued to hold.

'The assaulting companies at this time were highly disorganized, had no connection with their left and had no officers. It was then that the commanding officer Lt.Col.E.R. Mobbs D.S.O. and 2nd Lt.Berridge M.C. arrived in the front line. The former with a handful of men charged an enemy machine gun post and was seriously wounded. Before dying he wrote out a message to his battalion headquarters for reinforcements to be sent forward, and stated that he was seriously wounded, an act showing his devotion to duty at the last. The message, however, was never delivered.

THE MOBBS' OWN

'It must be stated that the capture of the first objective or blue line had been reported. This was correct as far as the battalion was concerned, but LOWER STAR POST on our left had not been captured. It had, however, been reported by walking wounded that the second objective (or the black line) had been captured.It was then that Colonel Mobbs decided to go forward and ascertain the position.

'Lt.Col.Mobbs' daring and extraordinary courage being known that he was restrained from leaving his headquarters for half an hour, but at the end of that time he definitely decided to go forward with a view to personally supervising the consolidation of the ground captured and for selecting a position for advancing battalion headquarters.

Before doing so he ordered 'B' company (reserve) to advance and occupy the consolidated JEER TRENCH.

'In a most critical situation when the two assaulting companies had lost all their officers, 2nd Lt.Berridge M.C. with the assistance of C.S.M.Afford and Sgt Twentyman reorganized the line and sent in a report to battalion headquarters. Upon receipt of this report 'D' company of the 13th Middlesex were sent forward to JEER TRENCH with special instruction to gain connections on the flanks. This company suffered heavy casualties in going forward and is reported to have crossed JEER TRENCH and later to have withdrawn and dug in between ILLUSIVE DRIVE and ILLUSIVE RESERVE, believing that none of our troops were in front of them.

'The trench mortar subsection also withdrew to that line and occupied a German trench mortar position

107

they believed to be the only one shown in arial photographs. Owing to LOWER STAR POST still being held by the enemy it was decided to withdraw our troops about the line of ILLUSIVE AVENUE and to consolidate strong positions on that line and establish communications with a Northampton strong point held and a further Leinster strong point.

An amended order was sent to O.C. 'D' company 13th Middlesex.

'2nd Lt. Berridge again went forward to effect the withdrawal, which he successfully accomplished, showing the upmost gallantry and dash, establishing a line of strong posts under heavy machine gun fire and shell fire. Several messages were sent back during this time when he was forward but did not reach battalion H.Q. the runners having lost their way. He reported personally afterwards.

'2nd.Lt.Berridge's work cannot be overestimated, and it was due to his efforts and devotion to duty that the situation was cleared.

'A carrying party was organised to take wire, sandbags, water and ammunition to the posts which had been established but it took many hours for them to find their way.

'Stretcher bearers have suffered heavy casualties so that the 12 reserve were sent for from the back area, and in the meantime, on account of the large number of wounded who were lying out, stragglers (men who had lost their way) were collected and displaced at the service of the medical officer. Many of these men did excellent work, and the greatest portion of the area was cleared by midnight.

'The relief of the battalion was partly carried out by the 1st North Staffords and partly by the 13th Middlesex, this was ordered on the zero evening. Runners went forward to bring in guides from the posts. This was just before dark. The runners failed to find the posts and the guids never arrived.

'It being considered unwise to carry out the relief by night it was not commenced until 4.00 a.m. the following day the 1st of August.

'Great credit is due to 2nd Lt's.Gorrings, Williams and Wild and the N.C.O.s and men with them in holding these posts during the night under heavy shell fire and in the most trying circumstances.

'During the morning of the 1st August the 1st North Staffs relieved the three right posts of the battalion and the 13th Middlesex relieved the posts on the left. The former had been formed on the 72nd brigade front when direction had been lost.

'It had rained incessantly throughout the operations and the men were thoroughly exhausted, wet through, and covered with mud.

'LOWER STAR POST. This proved to be the key point of the situation and was the cause of holding up the attack and preventing the final objective being taken.

'It is considered that the boundary between two units should not have passed so close to such a strong point, but that special assaulting troops should have been detailed to envelope the post.

'ZERO. If zero hour is during darkness, it is extremely difficult for the assaulting troops to keep proper direction and correctly extended lines. To ensure direction and correctly extended lines it should be that zero hour should be in daylight.

'STATE OF GROUND. Operations were undoubtedly handicapped by the bad conditions of the ground owing to severe weather which had existed previous to and on the 31st July. This also to a certain extent withheld the assaulting troops from keeping close in to our barrage, and the rate of advance of which is considered to have been too fast under the circumstances.

'REPORTS. A line of objective should not be reported as captured until it is ascertained that the flanks have been secured and communications obtained on the right and the left. It is dangerous to base reports on the statements of the wounded.

'MAP READING. The question of map reading and generally knowing ones position and finding the way at night, proved to be exceedingly difficult. This was principally due to the similarity of the ground and lack of landmarks. The use of a compass with a large scale, clearly contoured map would appear to have been the only measure to adopt. It is considered that the large Shrewsbury Forest map was adaptable to the circumstances.

'SANITATION. Latrine accommodation in CANADA TUNNELS was practically nil. No special latrines could be claimed and looked after by one battalion, because troops in the tunnel belonged to several regiments. It would have been advantageous if a Brigade sanitary squad had been organised to make and look after latrines. This would have probably decreased the large amount of urinating in the TUNNELS.'

Appended to this report of the action, was a tribute paid to the battalion by the Brigade commander:

THE MOBBS' OWN

SPECIAL ORDER.

I would like to place on record my very high appreciation of the splendid fighting qualities and gallantry of the officers N.C.O.'s and men who took part in the action of the 31st July 1917.

The enemy did his best to break up the attack and prevent us from gaining our objective, he employed his best troops for this purpose. His artillery and machine gun fire was heavy and intense during the advance the ground was ploughed up and boggy with shells. In spite of all these difficulties and opposition the 7th Battalion the Northamptonshire Regiment and the 2nd Battalion Leinster Regiment drove the enemy from his position on the high ground which the Brigade had been ordered to seize. Many officers were killed or wounded and the fight resolved itself into a soldier's battle which was won by extraordinary pluck and determination.

This was a performance of which troops may very well feel more than proud.

Brigadier General.

Commanding 73rd Infantry Brigade.

It can be noted in this report that Paddy Murphy had added a D.S.O. to his M.C. and had been promoted to command the Leinsters. Shortly after this action Lieutenant Colonel Murphy was killed by enemy shell fire.

Now that the time had arrived when the battalion could take stock of their action a casualty list was prepared. Once again it was clear on officer losses and very uncertain on the casualties among the other ranks. The stated officer casualties were as follows:

Officers killed: Lieutenant Colonel E.R.Mobbs. Second Lieutenant T.P.Litchfield. Missing: Second Lieutenants

111

L.H.Halliday and T.Ward.

Wounded: Captain A.O.Marshall. Lieutenants. S.H.Motion and A.F.R.George.

Second Lieutenants W.H.Cawston, F.L.Franklin, L.J.Laycock and A.H.Webb.

The losses in the ranks were: 37 killed, 162 wounded and 47 missing. A total of 246 men.

Because of the losses between the Northamptons and the Leinsters they joined ranks to form a composite battalion. Major Powell was promoted to the rank of Lieutenant Colonel to command the 7th Northamptons. No longer was this battalion formed of a majority of volunteers, no longer was it commanded by a former Kitchener man and never would be again.

Five

The people of Northampton had long been grieving their losses, now they had lost their hero, the one man that personified heroism, a Rugby player, who had become a distinguished soldier in such a short space of time. The reaction was immediate, a great sadness possessed the town and the local papers, followed by the Nationals, printed many tributes.

The 'Bedfordshire Times' gave particulars of how Edgar Mobbs met his death. 'The Times' in their turn printed a letter sent in by Second Lieutenant N.Spencer, who was a former pupil of Mobbs' old school Bedford Modern. It is easy having the benefit of hindsight and looking back at the florid prose of the time, to find it overtly dramatic and in this case rather questionable. Even so as a matter of historical interest, and as part of the Nation's respect for Edgar Mobbs the text of this letter is reproduced.

'I was F.O.O. in the stunt, and went over the top and saw Mobbs. Perhaps I was one of the last officers to speak to him. Anyway, my last sight of him is something that will be worth remembering of him. We had been waiting for three hours for the time to come, and the Boche shelled us terribly, and as for the rain, mud etc, well the papers will tell you all this. Then the minute came and we went forward through seas of mud and terrific shelling. The men were magnificent and our artillery under these new adverse conditions put up a barrage such as the Somme never saw.

'I was right behind Mobbs, introduced myself to him just before the hour as an old B.M.S. boy and talked about Bedford and R.C.Stafford. In the tornado of hostile shelling he got ahead, and seeing

113

a number of his men cut down by an undiscovered machine gun strong point, he charged it to bomb it certain death under such a terrific hail of shell and he went down.

'I have seen men, and good men, but for a man of his standing and his rank it was magnificent. I sat down afterwards in a captured post and, instead of that picture, I saw the old threequarter in his own 25 yards get the ball from a crumpled up scrum and get clean through and on. The same man, the same determination a born leader. Thank God for such men. I know that all who knew him, even in civilian days, which don't count at all will be glad of this picture of one of England's finest Rugby players in the greatest game a man can play. I am sure that Bedford will honour such a man, and not just put it in the paper. "Famous Rugby Player Killed." Long may the Modern turn out such men.'

In many ways this is a fitting and descriptive salute to Mobbs. In regard to the writer, he fails to explain why he was in the Northampton's area of combat. It is also difficult to comprehend how Colonel Mobbs would find time to have a chat about his old school in such trying conditions.

Teddy Cook a well known and respected Saint's player, then serving as a corporal in France wrote his own letter of appreciation:

'Dear Sir, It came as a very painful surprise to read in your valuable paper of the death in action of that great and gallant gentleman, Colonel E.R.Mobbs, D.S.O.

'It will for ever be a source of great pleasure to me that I spent the major portion of my Rugger career under his leadership. He was such a thorough sportsman. You will naturally understand that having such a long association in the world of sport with him, I feel his loss keenly. Therefore, it gives me great pleasure to know that the people of Northampton and sportsmen generally are going to do something for an everlasting memorial to him.

'Perhaps the following two incidents most fully illustrate his great thoughtfulness and give the reasons for him being so universally admired.

'The Saints had been away to play Devon Albion at Plymouth, and on their way back had to pass through Bristol on the Sunday, and, naturally, to while away the time some of the fellows were playing cards. E.R.M. on approaching the platform at Bristol happened to see a player's father who had come down to the station to have a few moments conversation with his son, and, feeling that he would not approve of card playing on a Sunday, immediately turned round and asked the players to stop until the train had passed through the station, which of course they did.

'The other incident occurred on a certain Saturday when the team was returning from a game with the United Services. One of the side had received a rather nasty kick on the head, and Edgar, although he had a most important engagement in the Town, would persist in seeing the player across to Euston although by doing so he made himself very late for his appointment.

'It is such actions as these, that he did daily, that made him so popular, at least in the world of sport and I have no doubt it was the same in his everyday life.'

Captain King who managed to obtain some leave back in Blighty, had a chat with the Independent and apart from repeating the details of the action, resulting in the loss of Edgar Mobbs, he did furnish some information which clearly shows

115

THE MOBBS' OWN

the type of man that he was. Captain King mentions that Edgar was only armed with his stick when he approached the enemy. No doubt the Mills bombs could not be readily seen in the darkness. Furthermore Edgar made no effort to conceal his badges of rank on his cuffs. This would be hardly necessary as his service dress would prove his officer rank as this applied to all officers at that time. Seeing that he was an officer the German gunners directed their fire upon him and hit him in the neck. Captain King claims that it took Edgar ten minutes to die, in which time he scribbled out his instructions.

The most humane aspect of Captain King's chat, was the information he imparted in connection with Edgar's orderly. He told his orderly, a man he was obviously close to, that this would be his last action, in fact he had been in action so many times that he had been ordered to stay in his headquarters. The divisional staff were aware of Edgar's worth and did not wish him to risk his precious life unduly.

A further article, based on an officer's letter, stated that Edgar was actually given permission by division to leave his headquarters, because of the critical situation his two companies found themselves in. During the early research for this book, the gentleman who had been Edgar's batman and no doubt the orderly in question, refused to speak on the matter apart from saying: 'All I'll say is that he was the bravest man in the British Army, and he was always good to me.'

Opinions will always differ, and very often the truth will remained veiled. The fact remains that Edgar had told his friend back in England that he would never again come home and he also told his orderly that he would not return. Bearing in mind that he was in poor health as a result of his wounds and suffering from persistent trench foot, was this a death wish? Many officers, and if it comes to that, many other ranks, suffered with breakdowns both mental and physical. Sergeant Boulter who won the Victoria Cross whilst serving with the

THE MOBBS' OWN

Northamptons, was commissioned and joined the 7th battalion. He had already suffered wounds carrying out the action that won him the V.C. With the 7th Northamptons he eventually collapsed with a heart attack. It must have been a hard and devasting life to be a hero. Was it all too much for Edgar?

In many respects some reluctance is found among veterans to speak freely about their war. To most it was a terrible experience they wished to forget. Even Colonel Berridge an undoubted hero, using the term in its true sense, had said that all he wanted to do when he got home was to forget. One soldier of the 7th, who lost an arm in his first hour in action, had a paranoid fear of relating his experiences, stating that he didn't wish to get into trouble. This was truly amazing, after all that time, and after loosing a limb this man was still subject to an inverted type of military discipline.

In this history there has been included many names. This has been done for a good reason. History is not made up from one man, as brave and as admired as that man undoubtedly was. The history of the 7th is made up from numerous men and their names have been added, so they can take their part in this history.

There is little doubt that Edgar Mobbs was well loved by his men. He treated them as a team and not a collection of other ranks. This in many ways made the 7th battalion, as it was then, unique. The following letter from a Royal Engineer who had served with him displays this devotion: ' By the death of Lieut.Colonel Mobbs, not only does Northampton lose a well known son, but England one of her bravest men.

> 'A finer specimen of an English gentleman or a more thorough sportsman never existed. We all knew his sterling qualities in the football field, and never were they seen to better advantage than in the Army. 'A born leader of men, Lieut Colonel Mobbs never spared himself. I have seen him in the trenches at all hours of the day or night, often wet to

THE MOBBS' OWN

the skin and covered in mud, but always cheerful with a word of encouragement for everyone, and he would visit dangerous points of the line whilst hesitating to send a subordinate.

'His one thought was the welfare of those under him, and without exception he was loved by all.

'No one but we that joined with him in 1914 knew what he did for us, continually getting us out of little scrapes, begging for extra leave, and a hundred other things during our period of training in England and helping us in every possible way when the real thing commenced.

'Like all brave men, he never advertised himself, never sought popularity, there was no need. His personality and example were sufficient.

'He had a hatred of red tape, and I remember an incident whilst we were in the trenches at St. Eloi over our knees in mud and water, in October 1915. Some officious indispensable in England returned a form stating that certain portions should be filled up with red ink. Captain Mobbs (as he was then) sent it back stating that red ink was scarce in the trenches, but that he would find plenty of blood, if that would do!

'I do not think any name is better known or more widely respected in the Army today than that of our late Colonel. I have hardly found anyone Canadians, Anzacs, South Africans or British troops who did not know him, nor did I hear anything but praise.

'We not only loved him, we looked up to him and boasted of him. We felt proud to belong to Mobbs' Regiment.

THE MOBBS' OWN

'He has gone, having given his life in that greatest of all causes, his county's sake, but so as that magnificent spirit of British sportsmanship and fairplay exists amongst us, so shall the name of Lieut. Colonel Mobbs never be forgotten by us or by our comrades from overseas.

'I know of no finer epitaph than: "He played the game."

'God rest his soul.'

As one of the letters indicated, the people of Northampton must do something for their fallen hero. The remarkable thing was that the war had not finished, but Edgar Mobbs was dead. Memorials were erected in every church and village, but that was after the armistice, not during this vast conflict which still had a tragic time to finish.

An appeal was made for the Edgar Mobbs' memorial fund and a committee was set up to deal with the contributions and to eventually come to terms with the many suggestions put forward. A memorial hall, a children's home, financing training for young Rugby players, the list was immense, and the contributions rolled in.

In the mean time the 7th battalion was still at the front fighting their war. They had been savaged by the loss of their Colonel and it must have been difficult for Colonel Powell to maintain the same type of spirit that had been within the battalion.

It was the usual trench duty, with men still being lost though various forms of enemy activity as they worked in the area of the Menin Road.

During September 1917 the battalion was shelled with mustard gas, but only had 6 men burnt.

On the 6th November 1917, the 7th selected a party to raid the enemy lines. The regimental diary described this action, which exemplifies the courage of every day soldiers in

119

THE MOBBS' OWN

following their orders.

'The battalion raided enemy lines at Bower Lane and Minnow, attempting to enter the Sap between these two points. There were two parties operating on the right and left of the Sap. A party of crawlers, Lance Corporal E.R.Hart and Private W.Skelton cut the wire near the junction of the right Sap within the German lines and entered the Sap. They found three Germans in a small dugout on the left side of the Sap as you look west. One man was left at the entrance. A double sentry post was then found in the Sap and the enemy spotted our crawlers. The crawlers shot both sentries. The noise aroused the Germans in the dugout and the man at the entrance threw a Mills bomb which killed all three occupants. On hearing the shots the party on the right Sap moved forward and found that the wire and mud were more difficult to negotiate than had been assumed. Before they could deliver the assault the enemy had reinforced in such numbers as to render the chances of success very small. The arrival of these reinforcements had compelled the crawlers to withdraw. Several hand grenades were thrown by the enemy but caused no casualties. In the mean time the crawlers on the left party had moved forward and were fired upon before they reached the enemy wire and were compelled to withdraw. The left attacking party made several attempts to get through and were held up by rifle fire and hand grenades. The party was then withdrawn.'

The climate of the war was altering, the Germans required a strategy that would severely weaken the allied armies, and possibly snatch a victory before the American army arrived with its potential economic strength and a vast reservoir of manpower. The Russian front had collapsed and the Bolsheviks withdrew Russia from the war. This released German divisions which could now be used on the Western Front.

On March the 21st there was a heavy morning mist, and the Germans attacked and broke through south of the Somme and were held back at Arras. This compelled Ludendorff, the German commander, to revise his plans and concentrate in breaking the allied hold of Arras.

The 7th battalion were in the line at Vraignes. The day prior to the German assault the battalion's C.O. and company commanders inspected the area the battalion would occupy. It was common knowledge that the enemy would attack in force, and the battalion was held in readiness to support the battalions already in the line.

At 4.30 in the morning of the 21st the enemy opened up with an intense bombardment. At 5.40 the 7th were ordered into the line. The companies were disposed in four redoubts covering the villages of Jeancourt and Vendelles and at the same time giving support to the troops of the 11th Infantry Brigade, who were meeting the enemy assault in front of La Verguir.

Owing to the persistent thick mist there was nothing to be seen and it was a nervous and anxious time for the 7th.

The line was penetrated by the German attack and the entire 66th division was pushed back to the redoubt which was held by 'B' company. The 27th Infantry Division held its line and maintained it throughout that night.

On the following day the Germans captured Le Verguier and the troops on the left flank of the battalion were falling back. Colonel Powell in his anxiety went over to the headquarters of the 17th Infantry Brigade in an attempt to clarify this critical position. On arriving he found the HQ was empty, the brigade had fallen back, leaving the 7th wide open to attack from the left flank. By 1.25 p.m. the 7th found that both their flanks were open and they were in isolation, separated from the rest of the brigade. Powell seeing that the 7th would be overwhelmed by the advancing enemy ordered his battalion to pull out and eventually came in contact with the 50th division which had been ordered to stem the German advance.

This type of action was repeated on the next day the 23rd. The battalion had taken up defensive positions in the village of Fez, and found that the troops on their left front were retiring and the enemy was advancing on their right. Orders came through that in an event of a general retirement the 7th were to take up positions on the high ground east of Falvy.

Fighting hard to hold their line, the battalion covered the withdrawal of the 3rd Rifle Brigade. Because of the exposed right flank, the enemy introduced field artillery and heavy machine gun fire. Being forced back by the sheer weight of the enemy, the battalion crossed the Somme river, where the bridges were blown up after them.

There was to be no respite for the Northamptons, they were then ordered to prepare for a counter attack, which was to be mainly operated by the French. The 7th went into the attack and found, much to their disgust that the French had not moved from their lines. The battalion quickly established a defensive position. Once again the enemy approached the open flanks and the 7th had to fall back to their original positions.

By this time the troops were tired and suffered many losses and orders came through that there should be a silent withdrawal to the village of Menaricourt. The Germans sent an attacking party of 300 to attack the position held by 'B' company, the Germans were fired upon by rifle and machine gun fire and 'B' company annihilated them.

The division on the left of the 7th were attacked and were compelled to retreat, once again leaving the 72nd Brigade's flank wide open. The Brigade attempted to cover their exposed areas and were thrown back. German infantry entered the line occupied by the 7th, mainly using hand grenades and well covered by their own machine guns. As it was

THE MOBBS' OWN

impossible to leave the trenches and attack the oncoming Germans due to their machine guns being on their flanks, the battalion found that the situation was critical, by this time they had used all their own hand grenades. Lewis guns were positioned and the companies managed to occupy rear trenches out of throwing range from the German grenades. They held out against considerable enemy strength until assisted by the 13th Middlesex who managed to retrieve one of the open flanks.

Moving through the 13th Middlesex 'B' and 'D' companies assisted in covering the retreat of the Brigade. The Brigade having been close to being captured pulled back across the river to safer ground.

There is no record of any casualties, either of officers or men. A few days after this action a draft of 386 men and 3 officers arrived to join the 7th, these figures possibly reflecting the losses.

During this time Powell had left the battalion to be replaced by S.S.Haynes who in turn was himself replaced by Leiutenant Colonel Grune. Gone where the days when the 7th lived under the aura of Edgar Mobbs.

The 7th were hit during the month of June by another enemy, this was flu' and the Army called it Pyrexia, 30 men went down with this vicious complaint. Within three days 3 officers and 80 men suffered from this outbreak. By the 22nd June 1918 over 200 men of the battalion were laid low with this flu' which had a greater effect upon the British Army than the Germans could manage.

A great deal of manpower had been lost by the Germans in their advance. This campaign had failed leaving both sides with a severe loss of men and a war tiredness.

Trench life returned to routine, with some activities taken on to relieve the men from the wretchedness and boredom of their daily duties. On the 6th August 1918 the battalion must have been short of nails needed for trench work, for the C.O.

organised a nail hunt and the men picked up 130lbs of nails in half an hour.

It is a tragedy, not confined to the 7th Battalion that one month before hostilities ceased the 7th lost a further 92 men in their final assault.

At last the time had arrived for the Armistice, when the firing had stopped and there would be no more casualties. The veterans were in a minority. There were few men left from the party who had gone to Shoreham with Edgar Mobbs. Others had served in other units and many had survived. It has been estimated that at least 80 of them came through the war. In time the service battalions were disbanded and the men went home. The 7th Service Battalion Nothamptonshire Regiment were awarded battle honours to be displayed on their colours. They were names of the battles in which the 7th participated with such gallantry: Loos, Hooge, Guillemont, Vimy Ridge, Messines, Battlewood, Pilkem Ridge, Cambria Maubeuge.

The distinguished record of the Battalion must be connected with that of Edgar Mobbs. There is little doubt that Edgar with his own personal charm and courage gave the 7th a lasting name. This does not detract from the efforts given by the other battalions of the regiment, they were unfortunate, for without a charismatic leader, who constantly invited the limited media of the time, they had little chance to match the reputation of the battalion that was truly Mobbs' own.

One of the tragedies emanated from this conflict is that Edgar's body was never found and consequently has no known grave. Once an attack had been finished, in the aftermath, the Germans would bury the dead on their side of the line within no mans' land. A small wooden cross would be pushed into the ground to denote a grave. Future artillery fire would destroy these crosses losing all trace of the dead.

The people of Northampton insisted that Edgar should be remembered by a substantial memorial in his name.

THE MOBBS' OWN

Mr.H.Manfield suggested a medal or a plaque should be placed in a church or a public building. This member of Parliament was obviously out of touch with the wishes of the people. The committee had to consider that the war was still on at that time and were oblivious to the tragedy of many local men also being killed. Should the memorial be devoted to Colonel Mobbs or to all the fallen?

As the debate carried on and subscriptions accumulated, the war finished. To mark this occasion and to salute the fallen a cenotaph was built and erected outside the CoOperative Stores in Abington Street as a temporary memorial. The people of Northampton still wanted a memorial that would be lasting and a tribute to the fallen of the town.

It was decided that a memorial should be commissioned and erected in the grounds of All Saints church, where it stands to this very day. This was in complete isolation to the Edgar Mobbs' fund, which was still under consideration. It was the time when the battalions were returning, very often represented by small detachments of men as battalion members were either serving in the Army of occupation in Germany or enjoying an early release. In reality the service battalions no longer existed.

The members of the committee governing the Mobbs' memorial and holding over one thousand five hundred pounds in donations, arranged a ceremony at the Mayor's Parlour. The president of the fund Lord Lilford was present, together with Edgar's father, Oliver Mobbs.

A handsome album containing the name of the major subscribers was presented to Oliver Mobbs. At this time, Edgar's father was partially paralysed and could not be expected to face a large assembly of donors, but agreed to meet the committee.

The album itself contained the Badge of the Northamptonshire Regiment, the Borough Arms, the County

THE MOBBS' OWN

Badge, the arms of Bedford Modern School and the badge of the East Midlands Rugby Union. The form of address contained in the album was as follows:

> 'Sir We ask your acceptance of this album containing the names of the subscribers to the memorial fund in honour of your gallant son. The contributors comprise admirers of his character and career from all parts of the world. The total sum raised spontaneously within a short period amounted to £2000, from which £500 was given to the East Midlands Union with which his name will ever be honourably associated and a silver challenge cup has been presented to Bedford Modern School, where he was educated.

'We sincerely hope that the sorrow of yourself and family in the loss of so noble a son is softened by the thought that it is shared by all who knew him and by the knowledge that his example will be an inspiration for future generations and his memory for ever cherished and enshrined in our annals as that of the men in every sphere who 'played the game,' and was faithful until death death that has been swallowed up in a glorious victory for the cause of civilisation.'

Lord Lilford made the presentation and gave a very short address. The major point being made that a great deal of subscribers who gave coppers to the fund, had not been mentioned and should not be forgotten. The 550 names in the album only represented one third of the people who had contributed.

Oliver Mobbs' reply could only be classed as excellent as he was a sick man facing a sad and exhausting time. He reminded the committee that Lord Lilford had presented his son with silver salver and silver cups in commemoration of his prowess as a football player some six years ago. He had no doubt that his son's training as a footballer fitted him for a soldier by strengthening his physique and knowledge of the control of men.

Because of Edgar's fame his father mentioned that he had admirers beyond our own country and generals in the field had testified to him being a born soldier.

> The most touching part of the address was in connection with the men who served under Edgar. 'What pleases me more than anything is that his men, not only looked up to him as a soldier, but they loved him because he always thought of them, rather than himself. I remember in letters he sent to me he used to describe how he had been round the trenches on snowy nights and arrived back at his dugout to find that it contained 4 inches of water. My son wrote to me "Dad, I am only doing my duty." His sense of duty however, was very large, in placing his own life before that of others and in giving so willingly for his country.'

Oliver Mobbs also mentioned the honour the press had allowed his son, starting with Mr.Holloway who obtained the interest of the national press. Special mention was made of the 'Sporting Life,' who conjured the phrase 'England's Edgar.'

There was further meeting and discussion on what shape the memorial should take and where it should be located. A further issue raised was over the principle that it should be a memorial to the 7th Battalion as well as Edgar Mobbs. This complication was not resolved for some considerable time.

During 1919 the sculptor Alfred Turner visited Northampton and was very impressed by the town's Market Square. This gentleman had been invited to meet the memorial committee to discuss his design for the Mobbs' Memorial. Because of this artists obvious fondness for the architectual structure of the Market Square it came as no surprise when it was suggested that the memorial should be sited at the south entrance of the square. The famous old green fountain, with its green metal structure that reminded people of a French public urinal did not escape

THE MOBBS' OWN

the criticism of Turner.

The memorial was going to be 18 feet high with a base 8 feet by 6 feet. On the summit of the memorial there would be a figure in bronze of the Goddess Of Fame, holding in one hand a laurel wreath and in the other a flaming torch. On the pedestal their would be a life size bust of Edgar Mobbs cast in bronze. On either side there would be representations of Edgar as a footballer and as a soldier.

Happily this design was accepted by the committee.

This memorial was built during the time that depression caused by economical failure hit the nation. Many of the veterans faced unemployment. Earl Haig who had already instigated the British Legion for the benefit of his former soldiers, gave a fitting example of its tragedy. He cited the story of one of his former Majors, a man decorated with the Victoria Cross, Distinguished Service Order and Military Cross, trudging the streets of London begging for a position.

It was a time for Industrial unrest and because of this the erection of the memorial was delayed for months. In time the memorial was ready to be placed in the Market Square.

It was in the month of July 1921 when the unveiling ceremony was held.

Many men of the old 7th battalion were present to pay homage to their fallen Colonel. Six member of the police force all Mobbs' men attended. The battalion's colours and colour party paraded. Colonel E.C.Bagnall and Major Guy Paget led 150 former members of the 7th.

The proudest moment was when the survivors of 'D' company marched through the town carrying a large wreath with the pronounced 'D' in the centre of its design. These 85 men were led by Major D.Farrar, Captain F.R.Berridge, D.S.O.,M.C., and 2 bars and Captain E.G.Passmore.

Many years have now passed. The Mobbs' memorial is visited each year by officials of the Rugby world, prior to their Mobbs' Memorial Game. At one time members of the battalion would attend, very few of them are now left to carry out this duty.

In the appendix to this book is the nominal roll of the 7th Battalion as it was on the 17th August 1915. It is hoped, in some small way, that this history will be a permanent memory to them.

Appendix.

Nominal roll of the 7th Battalion Northamptonshire Regiment as at the 17th August 1915. The roll is divided into companies and where men have lost their lives during the war, their date of death is included, together with their place of birth.

Due to the transfer of officers to other units, only a proportion of the listed officers continued to serve with the 7th Battalion. Officer casualties have been mentioned within the text. Regimental diaries would record the names of lost officers but not other ranks.

Roll of officers:

Lt.Col. A.Parkins. Majors: H.Walker Leigh, C.Bagnall, H.des Voeux, R.J.Bestink, J.W.Fisher, Captains: T.G.Paget, E.L.Mansfield, L.H.P.Birch, V.D.Short, R.C.Fowler, H.Wright, C.Hunt. Lieutenants: A.H.Flynn, E.R.Mobbs, D.Farrar, H.Grierson, J.L.Orquhart, H.King, R.Gurney, J.N.Morley, A.O.Marshall, J.C.Gurney, L.L.Phipps, S.H.Motion. Second Lieutenants: A.B.Cox,C.H. Martin, R.F.Houghton, C.L.Clarke, P.S.Hadley,S.C.Percival,F.A.Gurney,W.W.Taylor,R.D.Howett, J.L.A.Tyrell, E.G.Passmore, G.V.Nott, J.M.D.Hauntlett, T.Freeman, C.F.Saunders, H.M.Harvey, C.A.Debenham, H.Harris, H.P.Gill, A.W.Heaton, M.A.S.Vaile, B.N.Meadway, N.F.Palmer, A.H.B.Webster, D.W.Morris, A.Durrant Swan, G.K.Chatham, J.S.Harbottle, B.Wright, M.J.Selby, E.G.Butcher, R.P.E.Dale, L.P.Mortimer, C.H.Buckingham.

A Company.

R.Q.M.S. Cole, F.

C.S.M. Wait, Wm.

C.Q.M.S. Martin, W.E. Died of wounds 1/6/18. Sutton Bridge Lancs.

Sgt. Bailey, J. Died of wounds 28/4/17. Ilkstone, Derbyshire.
Sgt. Billingham, T.
Sgt. Love, C.R.
Sgt. Orton, H.
Sgt. Spring, W. Killed in action 18/8/16. Southwick, Northants.
Sgt. Stevens, J. Killed in action 31/7/17. St. Edmunds Northampton.
Sgt. Nunney, C.J.
Sgt. Smart, W.A.
Sgt. Chapman, B. Died of wounds 3/8/17. All Saints Northampton.
LSgt. Dickins, H.B.
LSgt. Bowell, H.J. Killed in action 27/9/15. Acton Middlesex.
LSgt. Lakey, Wm.
LSgt. Martlew, A.
Cpl. Beesley G.W.
Cpl. Warren, Wm.
Cpl. Kock, G.H.
Cpl. Jones, H.R.
Cpl. Freeman, R.
Cpl. Arnitt, J.C.
Cpl. Spence, A.H.
Cpl. Chadwick, J.
Cpl. Afford, Wm. H.
Cpl. Warren, E.
LCpl. Abbott, W.J.
LCpl. Anderson, T. Killed in action 18/8/16. Great Brington Northants.
LCpl. Beaumont J.J.
LCpl. Godfrey, P.C.
LCpl. Hog, A.C.
LCpl. Nash, R. Killed in action 18/8/16. Fulford Yorkshire.

THE MOBBS' OWN

LCpl. Thomas, A.H. Killed in action 29/6/16. Bath Somerset.
LCpl. Slark, C.H.
LCpl. Harod, W.
LCpl. Faulkner, C.S. Killed in action 27/9/15. Eastern Nesten Northants.
LCpl. Beadsworth, W.G. Killed in action 31/7/17. Bethnall Green Middlesex.
LCpl. Orpwood, S. Killed in action 23/7/18.(Military Medal.) Shiton Oxford.
LCpl. Broadbridge, C. E.
LCpl. Barber, F.S.
LCpl. Bond, A.
LCpl. Redley, Wm. Died of wounds 1/8/17. (Military Medal.) Kempston Beds.
LCpl. Rogers, A.
LCpl. Rogers, W.J.A.
LCpl. Nicholas, W.J.
LCpl. Meadows, T.M. Died of wounds 6/4/16. Thrussington Leics.
LCpl. Garfield, E.R.
LCpl. Hooper, W.R.
LCpl. Clift. J. N. Killed in action 18/8/16. Clerkenwell Middlesex.
LCpl. G.H. Batchelor.
LCpl. Bazeley, H.
Pte. Andrews. W.J.
Pte. Ayres, F.
Pte. Ambridge, W.
Pte. Abbott, A. Killed in action 18/8/16. Great Addington Northants.
Pte. Ashton, H.
Pte. Barnett, E.

THE MOBBS' OWN

Pte. Barnett, H.S.
Pte. Battison, H.
Pte. Beasley, Geo.
Pte. Bell. J.R.
Pte. Blakman, H.
Pte. Brice, J.
Pte. Briggs, P.
Pte. Britchford, W.G. Killed in action 27/9/15. Rothwell Northants.
Pte. Brown Jos. Killed in action 14/2/16. All Saints Northampton.
Pte. Brown, J.T.
Pte. Bull, B.
Pte. Bull, J.R.
Pte. Butcher, F. Killed in action 15/10/15. Towcester Northants.
Pte. Bugby, A. Died of wounds 16/6/16. Raunds Northants.
Pte. Barttlet, H.S.
Pte. Brinsley, J.
Pte. Botterill, H.
Pte. Bugby, Geo. W.
Pte. Brown. F.R.
Pte. Barrett, T.A. Killed in action 17/8/16. Great Weldon Northants.
Pte. Brightman, J. Killed in action 17/8/16. Northampton.
Pte. Chambers, H.
Pte. Childs, A.J.
Pte. Churchman, E.E. Pte. Clancy, C.E.
Pte. Clarke, C.
Pte. Clarke, F.D.
Pte. Clements, J.
Pte. Chapman, C.R.
Pte. Coe, A.

THE MOBBS' OWN

Pte. Coleman, C.E.
Pte. Collier, J. Killed in action 21/12/16. Darlington Durham.
Pte. Cook, S. Killed in action 17/8/16. St. Mary's Rushden.
Pte. Coulson, A.B.
Pte. Cousner, Geo.
Pte. Crofts, W. F.
Pte. Craddock, A. Killed in action 17/8/16. Earls Barton Northants.
Pte. Crane, J.A. Killed in action 19/4/17. St. Mary's Peterborough.
Pte. Cure, J.W.
Pte. Cooke, G.H.
Pte. Churchill, F.R.
Pte. Cornelius, J.E.
Pte. Cowley, A.L.
Pte. Crisp, A.
Pte. Chantrey, G.E. Died of wounds 12/10/16. St.John's Peterborough.
Pte. Churchill, S.T.
Pte Cooper, Fredk. Killed in action 18/8/16. Northampton.
Pte. Campion, G.E. Killed in action 17/8/16. Olney Bucks.
Pte. Day, E.T.
Pte. Deed, G.
Pte. Deane J.C.
Pte. Duffy, T.
Pte. Dunkley, H.
Pte. Dunkley, R. Killed in action 15/10/15. Pauler's Pury Northants.
Pte. Day, J.E.
Pte. Dray, G.H.
Pte. Dixon, G.
Pte. Deadman, E.H.W.

Pte. Dunkley, F.
Pte. Dawson, G.
Pte. Delamare, P.
Pte. Edis, F.
Pte. Errington, C.H.
Pte. Elliot, W.J.
Pte. Ewbank, T.G. Killed in action 18/8/16. Bermondsey Surrey.
Pte. Frankpitt, A. Killed in action 18/8/16. Exeter Devon.
Pte. Frisby, H.A.
Pte. Frisby, H.
Pte. Francis, A.J.
Pte. Faulkner, H. J.
Pte. Gardner, H.
Pte. Garrett, H.J.
Pte. Geary, W.
Pte. Gooderson, F.
Pte. Goom, R.H. Killed in action 13/4/17. Hammersmith Middlesex.
Pte. Green, H.G.
Pte. Green, J.
Pte. Gibbs, H.
Pte. Goodson, A. Killed in action 7/8/16. St. James Northampton.
Pte. Gill, G.S.
Pte. Gilby, A.
Pte. Hadsley, A.
Pte. Hales, F. Killed in action 18/8/16. Blackheath Kent.
Pte. Hallam, E.J. Killed in action 27/9/15. Battersea Surrey.
Pte. Hamilton, W.
Pte. Harrison, T.W.
Pte. Hart, F.E.

135

THE MOBBS' OWN

Pte. Hewkins, J. S.
Pte. Hill, Wm.
Pte. Hinks, F.A.
Pte. Hodson, F.J.
Pte. Holmes, Wm.
Pte. Holton, Wm.
Pte. Hook, S.A.
Pte. Harris, Thos. Killed in action 15/10/15. Swansea Glamorgan.
Pte. Holman, Wm. Killed in action 11/4/17. Little Bowden Northants.
Pte. Holton, T.S. Killed in action 18/8/16. Evenley Northants.
Pte. Housden, F. Killed in action 17/8/16. Sawtry Hunts.
Pte. Hewitt, E.J. Died of wounds 14/3/16. Hayford Northants.
Pte. Hensmen. J.J.
Pte. Hobden, J.
Pte. Johnson, J.
Pte. Jepson, C.H.
Pte. Keech, A.
Pte. King, A.E.
Pte. Kitcher, B.L.
Pte. Lane, G.
Pte. Lansbury, T.
Pte. Lane, G.H.
Pte. Leatherhead, J.
Pte. Lardner, E.
Pte. Lee, Wm, Killed in action 22/8/18. St. James Northampton.
Pte. Lickerish, H.A.
Pte. Ling, J.
Pte. Loasby, G. A.
Pte. Lovell, P.

THE MOBBS' OWN

Pte. Loveys, R.
Pte. Lumley, J.F.
Pte. Langley, H. Killed in action 18/8/16. Wellingborough Northants.
Pte. Lincoln, P.W.
Pte. Luckett, J.T.
Pte. March, R.R.
Pte. May, C.C. Died of wounds 2/8/17. Chertsy Surrey.
Pte. May J.T.H. Killed in action 12/4/17. Birmingham Warwick.
Pte. McPhun A.E. Killed in action 27/9/15. Salford Lancs.
Pte. Meadows, F. Killed in action 18/8/16. St. Marys Peterborough.
Pte. Marriot, C.
Pte. Miller, F.
Pte. Moore, P.B.
Pte. Manning, F. Killed in action 9/3/16. Brixworth Northants.
Pte. Money, G.W.
Pte. Moore, C.
Pte. Mould, J.E.
Pte. Northall, J.W.
Pte. O'Connor, W. Killed in action 31/7/17. West Ham Essex.
Pte. Osborn, C.
Pte. Palmer, A.H.
Pte. Panter, W.J.
Pte. Payne J.J.S.
Pte. Peacock, C.J.
Pte. Peck, W.A. Killed in action 17/8/16. Islington Middlesex.
Pte. Perkins, A.H.
Pte. Phillips, J.
Pte. Pittan, C. Died of wounds 18/8/16. Brackley Northants.
Pte. Price, A.V.

137

THE MOBBS' OWN

Pte. Randall, G.H.
Pte. Reeve, S. Killed in action 17/9/16. Spratton Northants.
Pte. Reynolds, C.F.
Pte. Reynolds, T.
Pte. Rivett, T.G.
Pte. Robinson, G.H.
Pte. Robinson, S.T.
Pte. Rowe, E.
Pte. Rooke, F.
Pte. Robinson, J.H.
Pte. Rowthorn, J.
Pte. Redley, Wm.
Pte. Sanders, E.J.
Pte. Steele, A.W.
Pte. Sheldrick, W. Killed in action 25/3/18. Walworth Surrey.
Pte. Slark, P.
Pte. Smith, S. C.
Pte. Smith, B.
Pte. Smith, T. Killed in action 25/3/18. Paulers Pury Northants.
Pte. Southorn, W.
Pte. Spencer, J.H.
Pte. Spriggs, Wm.
Pte. Stanton, H.
Pte. Stapely, W.S.
Pte. Stephenson, W.A.
Pte. Stevens, H.E.
Pte. Stanley, W.
Pte. Sturgess, G.E.
Pte. Swan, A.J.
Pte. Steene, F.O. Died of wounds 15/8/16. Vauxhall Middlesex.
Pte. Smith, G.H.P.

Pte. Templeman, R.
Pte. Thompsett, D.
Pte. Timms, G. Killed in action 19/6/17. Northampton.
Pte. Tite, A.M. Killed in action 17/8/16. Leicester.
Pte Trowell, G.
Pte. Tucker, H.
Pte. Tuckey, J. Killed in action 31/7/17. Brackley Northants.
Pte. Thompson, O.
Pte. Thomson. S.
Pte. Tyler, Wm. Killed in action 17/8/16. Brayfield Northants.
Pte. Varnham, W. Killed in action 21/3/18. (Distinguished Conduct Medal) Egham Surrey.
Pte. Thurlow, G. W.
Pte. Walker, H.
Pte. Waples, O.
Pte. Ward, G.W.
Pte. Watts, F.
Pte. Winn, F.C.
Pte. Ward, L.
Pte. West, A.
Pte. Wells, C.J. Died of wounds 30/3/16. Earls Barton Northants.
Pte. West, W. Died.3/11/17.(Military Medal) Stoke Goldington Bucks.
Pte. White, H.W.
Pte. Whitehead, W.
Pte. Whiting, F.
Pte. Williams, H.
Pte. Williams, J.L.
Pte. Williams. W.J.
Pte. Wood, E. Died of wounds 18/2/18. Harpole Northants.
Pte. Wright, A.
Pte. Webster,T.S.

THE MOBBS' OWN

Pte. Wardiell, J.B.
Pte. Warren, A. Killed in action 18/8/16. Moulton Northants.

B Company.

C.S.M. Drage, W.
C.Q.M.S. Wix, A.G.
CSgt. Bounds, B.
Sgt. Bedford, E.
Sgt. Coles, J.W.
Sgt. Moss, W.
Sgt. Tomlinson, J.P.
Sgt. Gray, W.T.
Sgt. Young, T.G. Killed in action 27/2/15. Stanway Essex.
Sgt. Hart, A.G.H.
Sgt. Baxter, C.F.
LSgt. Allen, A.G. Killed in action 27/9/15. Woodford Northants.
LSgt. Baxter, Killed in action 27/9/15. Kettering Northants.
LSgt. King, A.E.
LSgt. Marlow, J.A.
Cpl. Baxter, G. F.
Cpl. Sheere, A.
Cpl. Green, M.V. Died 27/9/15. Writtle Essex.
Cpl. Jackson, A. Killed in action 27/9/15. Watlington Norfolk.
Cpl. Mackerness, F.H.
Cpl. Worrall, W.
LCpl. Brookman, J.
LCpl. Hodge, D.
LCpl Seddon, E.J.
LCpl. Smith, F. Killed in action 18/8/16. Wymington Beds.
LCpl. Sherratt, C.H.
LCpl. Simpson. J.R.
LCpl. Edwards, F.

THE MOBBS' OWN

LCpl. Holdway, C.H. Killed in action 17/8/16. Lambeth Surrey.
LCpl. Bursill, C.A. Died of wounds 21/4/16. Islington Middlesex.
LCpl. Buswell, A.C. Killed in action 27/9/15. Northampton.
LCpl. Hammond, J.W. Died of wounds 24/1/17. Chiswick Middlesex.
LCpl. Mackness, R.
LCpl. Tomblin,
L. LCpl. Vipan, F.
LCpl. Knight, H.J. Killed in action 16/6/17. Gretton Northants.
LCpl. Jones, J.T.
LCpl. Parish, E.G.
LCpl. Gibbons, H.J.
LCpl Johnson, T.
Pte. Abbott, J.
Pte. Addy, T. Killed in action 17/8/16. Newark On Trent Staffs.
Pte. Alexander, R.
Pte. Ashford, Wm. Killed in action 18/8/16. Kingsthorpe Northampton.
Pte. Arnett. J. H. Killed in action 27/9/15. Polebroke Northants.
Pte. Baden, Wm. Killed in action 25/9/15. Marylebone Middlesex.
Pte. Bailey, G.H.
Pte. Bannister, T.
Pte. Bates, F.R.
Pte. Barnard. W. Killed in action 27/9/15. Southwick.
Pte. Barnes, F.
Pte. Bedford, H. Killed in action 27/9/15. Yardley Hastings Northants.
Pte. Bessley, F.
Pte. Berrill, A.S.
Pte. Berry, E.

141

THE MOBBS' OWN

Pte. Bannard, L.
Pte. Bird, G.F.
Pte. Brown, T.
Pte. Boon, R. Killed in action 13/11/15. Gretton Northants.
Pte. Britten, C.H.
Pte. Broadfield, R. H.
Pte. Brown, A.
Pte. Brown, W.A. Killed in action 27/9/15. Rugeley Staffs.
Pte. Brown, F. Killed in action 27/9/15. Pauler's Pury Northants.
Pte. Brown, Wm. Died 7/10/15. Pauler's Pury Northants.
Pte. Burnham, H.
Pte. Burton, P.
Pte. Bellamy, E.A.
Pte. Braggins, C.
Pte. Betts, B.J. Killed in action 17/8/16. St. Martins Northampton.
Pte. Boyles, W.G. Died of wounds 10/3/16. Farthinghoe Northants.
Pte. Berridge, H.
Pte. Beesley, F.J.
Pte. Barby, K.E.
Pte. Baxter, J.E. Killed in action 21/10/15. Wellingborough Northants.
Pte. Bedford, S.G.
Pte. Carter, C. Killed in action 25/9/15. Northampton.
Pte. Castle, S.
Pte. Coit, W.C.
Pte. Coleman, E.
Pte. Collins, E.
Pte. Conquest, G.S.
Pte. Cook, Wm.
Pte. Copus, A,

THE MOBBS' OWN

Pte. Cowley, H.E. Killed in action 27/9/15. St. Marys Rushden Northants.
Pte. Croft, C.F. Killed in action 27/9/15. Wilbarston Northants.
Pte. Cross, Wm. Killed in action 14/2/16. Nottingham.
Pte. Crossman, A.
Pte. Crowhurst, H.
Pte. Chamberlain, F.
Pte. Carvell, B.G.
Pte. Coulson, M. Killed in action 27/9/15. Polebrook Northants.
Pte. Chambers, G.R.
Pte. Cross, C.
Pte. Coles, T.E.
Pte. Coleman, L.
Pte. Cox, J.
Pte. Culverhouse, T.H. Killed in action 10/12/16. Northampton.
Pte. Davies, E.
Pte. Denton, W.A.
Pte. Downing, S.J.
Pte. Dunkley, C.
Pte. Drage, W.R.
Pte. Davies, M.G.
Pte. Eakland, G.
Pte. Eyles, J.T.
Pte. Edghill, H.
Pte. Ellard, G.W. Killed in action 25/9/15. St Matthews Northampton.
Pte. Fender, G.
Pte. Fisher, E.
Pte. Finnis, P.V. Killed in action 8/2/17. Mile End Middlesex.
Pte. Fletcher, E.J. Died of wounds 27/3/18. Southwark Surrey.
Pte. Flint. J. H.

143

THE MOBBS' OWN

Pte. Flowers, W.
Pte. Foster, A.H. Killed in action 25/3/16. West Ham Essex.
Pte. Fursdon, R.
Pte. Faulkner, J.T. Killed in action 27/9/15. Holcott Northants.
Pte. Fellows, G.T.
Pte. Frost, H.
Pte. Fellowes, Wm.
Pte. Gamage, E.
Pte. Goode, J.
Pte. Goude, R.
Pte. Gouldby, J.E.
Pte. Gillham, C.
Pte. Hale, A.T.
Pte. Halliday, C.H.
Pte. Heather, E.R.
Pte. Hemmings, A.S. Killed in action 10/3/16. Fulham, Middlesex.
Pte. Hepworth, Wm.
Pte. Holloman, G.
Pte. Howson, W.
Pte. Hamilton, A.
Pte. Higginbottom, J.T.
Pte. Hensher, C. J. Killed in action 23/3/16. Tooting Surrey.
Pte. Hope, W. Died of wounds 9/11/15. Hammersmith Middlesex.
Pte. Irons, W. Killed in action 27/9/15. Weedon Northants.
Pte. Ives, C. Died of wounds 24/8/16. Bayswater Middlesex.
Pte. Iliffe, F.A. Killed in action 18/6/17. Thrapston Northants.
Pte. Incles, F.
Pte. Jackson. J.T.
Pte. Jeggo, E.H.
Pte. Jinks,C.

Pte. Jones, F.
Pte. Jones, F. Killed in action 17/8/16. Stratford Essex.
Pte. King, B.
Pte. King, W.J.
Pte. King, E. Died of wounds 31/8/16. Irthlingborough Northants.
Pte. Knight, A.C. Killed in action 29/9/15. Hardingstone Northants.
Pte. Knighton, W.
Pte. Kirby, F.J.S.
Pte. Kite, G.L.
Pte. Kilsby, A.
Pte. Lammerton, H.H.
Pte. Lammerton, W.G. Died of wounds 27/7/16. Sandwich Kent.
Pte. Leggett, E.E. Killed in action 16/6/17. Sweffling Suffolk.
Pte. Leversha, T.T. Killed in action 27/9/15. Bridgwater Somerset.
Pte. Lewis, T.W. Died of wounds 15/3/16. Hoxton Middlesex.
Pte. Lovell, W.
Pte. Lull, A.
Pte. Lunn, C.H.
Pte. Liddington, F.
Pte. Leeson, G.W
Pte. Magee, M.
Pte. Martin, W.
Pte. Maskell, A.
Pte. Mason, E.
Pte. Matthie, F. Killed in action 18/8/16. Chelsea Middlesex.
Pte. McFarlane, P.
Pte. Masters, T.
Pte. Moore, A.

THE MOBBS' OWN

Pte. Muggleton, J.H. Killed in action 27/9/15. Wilbarston Northants.
Pte. Munton, W.E.
Pte. Miller, W.A.
Pte. Miles, E.
Pte. Mander, F.
Pte. Noon, A.
Pte. Noon, J.
Pte. Northern, S.
Pte. Newton, C.H.
Pte. Nash, J.
Pte. Orpwood, E.J.R. Killed in action 27/9/15. Shilton Oxford.
Pte. Osborne, C.
Pte. Palmer, G.A.
Pte. Payne, J.
Pte. Perrell, J.H.
Pte. Pettitt, H.T.
Pte. Poulson, F.G.
Pte. Price, A.T. Killed in action 27/9/15. Stratford Essex.
Pte. Pratt, R.
Pte. Pugh. F.
Pte. Putman, H.
Pte. Pattenden, J. Died of wounds 18/10/15. Slaugham Sussex.
Pte. Payne, H.
Pte. Pickering, F.
Pte. Prior, R.
Pte. Parrott, J.T.
Pte. Phipps, F.J. Killed in action 27/9/15. Northampton.
Pte. Ratcliffe, J.F.J. Died of wounds 27/9/15. Stony Stratford Bucks.
Pte. Renant, R.G. Killed in action 29/6/16. Southwick Northants.

THE MOBBS' OWN

Pte. Ribbitts, C.J.
Pte. Richardson, F.
Pte. Robinson, S.F.
Pte. Rose, C. Killed in action 17/8/16. Richmond Surrey.
Pte. Rubens, C.J. Died of wounds 27/3/18. Hackney Middlesex.
Pte. Ratley, E.
Pte. Raynor, D.
Pte. Robinson, P.
Pte. Richards, J.L. Killed in action 27/9/15. Kettering Northants.
Pte. Sanderson, F.
Pte. Sharman, A.L.
Pte. Sherratt, A.J.
Pte. Sibley, S.
Pte. Smallpiece, R.W.
Pte. Smeeton, F. Killed in action 27/9/15. St. Crispins Northampton.
Pte. Smith, A.E. Killed in action 17/8/16. Walworth Surrey.
Pte. Smith, T.
Pte. Smith, J.
Pte. Stevens, J.
Pte. Spencer, C. Killed in action 18/8/16. St. Andrews Northampton.
Pte. Spendlove, J. Killed in action 27/9/15. Gretton Northants.
Pte. Spendlove, L.
Pte. Springwell, T.
Pte. Steventon, J.H.
Pte. Staughton, E.J. Killed in action 27/9/15. Little Paxton Hunts.
Pte. Streeton, A. Killed in action 27/9/15. Earls Barton Northants.
Pte. Styles, A.L.
Pte. Swain, E.J.
Pte. Simsey, T.W.

THE MOBBS' OWN

Pte. Smith C.H. Killed in action 25/3/18. Dodford Northants.
Pte. Talbot, H.
Pte. Taylor, G.A.
Pte. Taylor, R.
Pte. Teeboon, G.
Pte. Teeboon, R.
Pte. Thompson, J. Killed in action 17/8/16. Pitsford Northants.
Pte. Timms, F.
Pte. Tornberg, E.
Pte. Trickey, A.
Pte. Toone, Wm.
Pte. Trinder, W.A.
Pte. Trusler, A.
Pte. Turland, C. Killed in action 27/9/15. Overstone Northants.
Pte. Thompson, C.
Pte. Tate, J.D.
Pte. Thornton, W.T.
Pte. Tuckey, A.G. Killed in action 27/9/15. Brackley Northants.
Pte. Underwood, F.M.
Pte. Willis, C.
Pte. Walker, C. died 27/12/16. Northampton.
Pte. Walker, S.T.
Pte. Watson, W.R. Died 25/7/18. Rushden Northants.
Pte. Weekly, H.
Pte. West, F.C. Killed in action 27/9/15. Epping Essex.
Pte. West, J.W.
Pte. Wilcox, A.
Pte. White, A. Killed in action 25/3/18. Sepulchres Northampton.
Pte. Wingrove, W.E. Died of wounds 29/6/16. Barnsbury Middlesex.

Pte. Wood, T.
Pte. Wootton, G.
Pte. Wright, H.
Pte. Wrighton, C. Killed in action 19/8/16. Aynho Northants.
Pte. Wyman, C.
Pte. Young, W. Killed in action 19/6/17. All Saints Northampton.

C Company.

C.S.M O' Connell, P. Killed in action 27/9/15. Cork Ireland.
C.Q.M.S. Saunders, C.
Sgt. Barnes, W.G.
Sgt. Chivers, J.
Sgt. Newman, T.H.
Sgt. Ward, B.
Sgt. Gale, H. Killed in action 25/9/15. St. Marys Peterborough.
Sgt. Wenn, B.C.
Sgt. Hill, C.G.
LSgt. Boyson, T.
LSgt. Smith, F.W.
LSgt. Hunting, N.R.
LSgt. Harrison, C.
LSgt. Kinns, T.
Cpl. Jordon. J.L.
Cpl. Lawford, J.
Cpl. Armstrong, J.L. Died of wounds 28/10/15. St. Marys Peterborough.
Cpl. Ellis, A.
LCpl. Bird, G.C.
LCpl. Blair, Wm. Killed in action 25/9/15. Camberwell Surrey.
LCpl. Bunyan, E.E.
LCpl. Church, E.S.
LCpl. Furniss, R.M.

LCpl. Hubbard, W. Died of wounds 15/10/15. St. Marys Peterborough.
LCpl. Jacques, J.
LCpl. Jameson, R.R.
LCpl. Vergette, J.
LCpl. Wilford, L.
LCpl. Watling, J.
LCpl. Franklin, G.
LCpl. Reedman, A.
LCpl. Whittle, W.J.
LCpl. Battams, W.H. Killed in action 25/9/15. Shutlanger Northants.
LCpl. Moules, W.H. Killed in action 18/8/16. St. Peters Northampton.
LCpl. Wilford, W.G.
LCpl. Newell, A.C.
LCpl. Reed, C.G.
LCpl. Foster, H.
LCpl. Wilson, N.
LCpl. Cuthbert, C.H.
Pte. Allday, F.L. Killed in action 25/9/15. Aston Warwick Northants.
Pte. Allebone, W.
Pte. Allen, T.D.
Pte. Askew, T. Killed in action 27/9/15. St. Johns Peterborough.
Pte. Allen, W.
Pte. Askew, T.
Pte. Allen, W.
Pte. Barber, C.W.
Pte. Barry, J.
Pte. Barnes, F.W. Killed in action 17/8/16. Newborough Northants.

THE MOBBS' OWN

Pte. Bazeley F. Died of wounds 20/9/16. Sibbertoft Northants.
Pte. Beales, A.E.
Pte. Berrisford, F.
Pte. Bettles, G.J.
Pte. Blott, G.H.
Pte. Brains, A.E.
Pte. Bodger, B.H. Killed in action 27/9/15. Elton Hunts.
Pte. Bradshaw, F. Killed in action 27/9/15. St. Marys Peterborough.
Pte. Brains, C. Killed in action 27/9/15. Woodford Northants
Pte. Brian, D.
Pte. Briers, G.
Pte. Bright, J.T.
Pte. Brown, A.E.
Pte. Brunswick, C.G.
Pte. Bull, J.F.
Pte. Bunning, C.H.
Pte. Birks, J.V.
Pte. Burroughs, H. Killed in action 23/6/16. Walworth Surrey.
Pte. Burton, A.
Pte. Butler, G.
Pte. Barnes, P.
Pte. Brown, A.
Pte. Brown, H.
Pte. Butts, J.T.
Pte. Butler, J.R.E. Killed in action 27/9/15. All Saints Peterborough.
Pte. Barnes, R. Killed in action 25/3/18. Walton Northants.
Pte. Blunt, G.
Pte. Bower, T.H.
Pte. Chapman, Wm.

THE MOBBS' OWN

Pte. Charlton, A.
Pte. Cobley, J.T. Killed in action 29/9/15. Maxey Northants.
Pte. Colbert, D. Killed in action 27/9/15. Orton Northants.
Pte. Coles, J.T.
Pte. Collins, E.C.
Pte. Cooper, R.P.
Pte. Cowley, F.
Pte. Cracknell, L.
Pte. Crick, G.
Pte. Crowder, E.
Pte. Cunnington, C.
Pte. Cussens, A.M.
Pte. Coley, J.G.
Pte. Clements, H.A.
Pte. Clarke, J.
Pte. Curtis, E.P.
Pte. Crop, R.
Pte. Cowley, J.G.
Pte. Clements, A.
Pte. Calcutt, A.H.
Pte. Dale, G.
Pte. Day, H.
Pte. Dell, C.
Pte. Ding, E.A.
Pte. Dowson, J.C.
Pte. Draper, W.E.
Pte. Faulkner, W.F.
Pte. Franks, W.
Pte. Frost, S.H. Killed in action 27/9/15. Colchester Essex.
Pte. Gardner, W.J. Killed in action 27/9/15. London.
Pte Garner, A.D.

THE MOBBS' OWN

Pte. Cathercole, E.J. Killed in action 27/9/15. March Cambs.
Pte. George, F.W.
Pte. George, H.
Pte. Gilbert, H. Died 14/10/16. St. Marys Rushden.
Pte. Guides, J.E.
Pte. Goodwin, A.
Pte. Gordon, W.C.
Pte. Green, H.
Pte. Green, J.A.
Pte. Groom, C.R.
Pte. Gubbins, B.
Pte. Gudgeon, M.
Pte. Gunn, H.
Pte. Goulty, H.
Pte. George, C.H.
Pte. Gray, Wm.
Pte. Holland, G.H.
Pte. Hill, H.E.
Pte. Hall, A.W.
Pte. Hall, J.
Pte. Hall, H. Killed in action 29/9/15. Stewkley Beds.
Pte. Hare, S.T. Died of wounds 19/8/16. Shoreditch Middlesex.
Pte. Haynes, S. Killed in action 27/9/15. Selby Yorkshire.
Pte. Herbert, A.S Killed in action 27/9/15. Nassington Northants.
Pte. Hill, P. Killed in action 27/9/15. St. Johns Peterborough.
Pte. Hitchcock, H.G.
Pte. Hopkins, C.H.
Pte. Hornsby, S.J.
Pte. Hotchen, C.A. Killed in action 27/9/15. Potter Hanworth Lincs.

Pte. Houghton, W. Killed in action 27/9/15. Holcot Northants.
Pte. Hunt. W.G.
Pte. Hilliard, A.H. Killed in action 27/9/15. Elton Hunts.
Pte. Harrison, J.H. Died 14/12/15. West Deeping Lincs.
Pte. Holmes, A. Killed in action 27/9/15. Eye Northants.
Pte. Howes, H. Killed in action 18/8/16. Hartford Hunts.
Pte. Ingamells, W. Killed in action 27/9/15. Fletton Hunts.
Pte. Jackson, C.C. Killed in action 6/7/16. St. Marys Rushden Northants.
Pte. Jackson, J.W.
Pte. Jolly, R.
Pte. Jones, C. Killed in action 18/8/16. Bozeat Northants.
Pte. Jordon, F.
Pte. Jordon, G.
Pte. Johnson, C.W. Died of wounds 5/10/15. Croft Lincs.
Pte. Kentish, C.
Pte. Lane, J.
Pte. Lawrence, W.R.
Pte. Leech, F. Killed in action 26/9/15. Earls Barton Northants.
Pte. Lock, E.J. Killed in action 27/9/15. Fletton Hunts.
Pte. Law, D. Killed in action 27/9/15. St. Andrews Northampton.
Pte. Lock, N.
Pte. Mabbutt, J.W.
Pte. Mantle, J.B.
Pte. Maddocks, D.
Pte. Marsh, G.W.
Pte. Measures, I. Killed in action 27/9/15. St. Marys Peterborough.
Pte. Mills, W.J.
Pte. Minney, Wm.
Pte. Moore, C.
Pte. Morris, F.

THE MOBBS' OWN

Pte. Mumford, E.F.
Pte. Meadows, E.S.
Pte. Merchant, E.M. Died of wounds 9/8/17. Peterborough.
Pte. Munns, H. Killed in action 31/7/17. Ramsey Hunts.
Pte. Marshall, A.V. Killed in action 27/9/15. Perth Australia.
Pte. Marlow, J. Killed in action 27/9/15. Desborough Northants.
Pte. Noon, F.
Pte. Nettlingham, W.G. Died of wounds 20/8/15. Cowley St. John Oxford.
Pte. Newberry, R.W.
Pte. Noble, E.
Pte. Noon, J.
Pte. Oakley, T. Killed in action 27/9/15. Elton Hunts.
Pte. Osborn, F.W.
Pte. Pack, E.
Pte. Papworth, B.
Pte. Parkins, R.H. Killed in action 17/4/17. St. Marys Peterborough.
Pte. Parrott, G. Killed in action 10/2/16. Yaxley Hunts.
Pte. Percival, H.W.
Pte. Perkins. C.
Pte. Phillips, W.P. Killed in action 17/8/16. Woodston Hunts.
Pte. Poole, T.
Pte. Presley, F.
Pte. Prior, J.
Ptc. Pollard, A.
Pte. Pywell, E.
Pte. Poole, W. Died of wounds 31/7/18. St. Pauls Peterborough.
Pte. Rands, T.E.
Pte. Rimes, T.A.
Pte. Rawlings, A. Killed in action 27/9/15. St. Marys Peterborough.

Pte. Robinson, J.R. Killed in action 27/9/15. Holme Hunts.
Pte. Robinson, R.C. Killed in action 27/9/15. Irchester Northants.
Pte. Redhead, A.
Pte. Roden, G.
Pte. Russell, A.H.
Pte. Rusted, E.L. Killed in action 27/9/15. Bassingbourn Herts.
Pte. Rimes, A.S. Killed in action 25/3/18. Churwell Yorks.
Pte. Royce, J. Killed in action 27/9/15. Gunby Lincs.
Pte. Sabin, W.
Pte. Sadler, A.
Pte. Sanders, J.T.
Pte. Sanderson, H.
Pte. Sayers, J.A. Killed in action 27/9/15. St. Pancras Middlesex.
Pte. Schofield, H.
Pte. Shelton, J.
Pte. Sherry, S.R.
Pte. Simpson, G. Killed in action 27/9/15. Peterborough.
Pte. Smith, G.C. Killed in action 27/9/15. Essendine Lincs.
Pte. Smith, H.
Pte. Smith, J.
Pte. Sprigg, C.E.
Pte. Smith, W. Killed in action 27/9/15. Peterborough.
Pte. Spencer, G.
Pte. Stanford, W.F. Killed in action 29/9/15. St. Johns Peterborough.
Pte. Stead, J.W.
Pte. Strickland, J.
Pte. Stuckbury, H.
Pte. Swiffen, H.
Pte. Stanton, W.
Pte. Spriggs, R.

Pte. Scott, A. Killed in action 27/9/15. Oakham Rutland.
Pte. Smith, E.W.
Pte. Spencer, T. Killed in action 31/7/17. Elton Hunts.
Pte. Tansey, J.T.
Pte. Thompson, A.C.
Pte. Thompson, C. Killed in action 27/9/15. Oldland Common Glos.
Pte. Townsend, H.
Pte. Turner, F.
Pte. Tyler, R.T. Died of wounds 30/9/15. St. Johns Peterborough.
Pte. Tomkins, R.G.
Pte. Underwood, J.
Pte. Walker, J.
Pte. Watts, P.F. Killed in action 15/10/15. Woodston Hunts.
Pte. Weekley, E. H
Pte. Whiteman, W. Killed in action 27/9/15. Raunds, Northants.
Pte. Whitwell, H. Killed in action 19/4/17. Werrington Northants.
Pte. Wilkinson, H.W. Killed in action 6/2/17. Sibbertoft Northants.
Pte. Wills, A.E.
Pte. Wise, E.T.
Pte. Wright, C.
Pte. Wenn, S.R.
Pte. Wilkin, R.
Pte Wilford, W.C.
Pte. Ward, F.

D Company.

R.S.M. Carter, W.
C.S.M Neil, W. Killed in action 27/9/15. St Johns Westminster Middlesex.

157

THE MOBBS' OWN

S.M. Harbour, J.W.
C.Q.M.S. Lodge, F.D.S.
CSgt. Hitch, F.H.D.
SgtDmr. Allen, F.T.
Sgt. Bailey, F.
Sgt. Booth, F.
Sgt. Pettit, H.
Sgt. Stock, J. Killed in action 27/9/15. St. Pauls Northampton.
Sgt. Ayris, H.
Sgt. Vernon, C.T.
Sgt. Jackson, W.
Sgt. Ruston, A.M.
Sgt. Maddock, T.
Sgt. Brown, H.W.
LSgt. Crick, W.
LSgt. Payne, F.
LSgt. Harding, J.H. Killed in action 2/9/16. St. Pauls Northampton.
LSgt. Titley, J. Killed in action 27/9/15. Hawkhurst Kent.
LSgt. Adkins, F.E.
Cpl. Affleck, H.
Cpl. Bennett. W.B. Died 26/8/16. Bourn Lincs.
Cpl. Hayward, P.G.
Cpl. Smith, A.G.
Cpl. Buswell, E.W.
Cpl. Marriot, C.
Cpl. Fraser, H.
Cpl. Smith, C.W.B. Killed in action 18/8/16. Rushden Northants.
LCpl. Betts, A.F. Killed in action 27/9/15. St. Sepulchres Northampton.
LCpl. Green, C.

THE MOBBS' OWN

LCpl. Holden, A.C. Died of wounds 10/6/16. St. Lawrence Northampton.
LCpl. Lawson, J.F.
LCpl. Ormrod, F.
LCpl. Pebody, H.
LCpl. Perkins, G.W. Killed in action 17/11/15. Higham Ferrers Northants.
LCpl. Phillips, D. Died of wounds 24/11/15. Abington Cambs.
LCpl. Rushton, R.E.
LCpl. Willett, H.
LCpl. Gillam, J.G. Killed in action 27/9/15. Cleeve Prior Worc.
LCpl. P. Spanton, P.
LCpl. Dimblebee, C.W.
LCpl. King, O.C. Killed in action 25/9/15. Thurleigh Beds.
LCpl. Butcher, F.
LCpl. Farr, P.
LCpl. Garrett, S.P.
LCpl. Taylor, W.C.
LCpl. Sturgess, R.
LCpl. McCullagh, C.
LCpl. Redhead, H.W. Killled in action 27/9/15. Cranford Northants.
LCpl. Roberts, L.J.
LCpl. Workman, C.H. Killed in action 27/9/15. Kentish Town Middlesex.
LCpl. Baxter, S.
Pte. Squires, E. Died 4/9/16. Christ Church Northampton.
Pte. Adams, S.
Pte. Addington, A.
Pte. Alibone, A.E. Killed in action 17/8/16. (Distinguished Conduct Medal.) St. Edmunds Northampton.
Pte. Allison, V.B.

159

THE MOBBS' OWN

Pte. Amos, E.
Pte. Ashton, F.J.
Pte. Axford, F.H. Killed in action 18/8/16. London.
Pte. Bailey, J.G.
Pte. Bament, C.
Pte. Bass, F.W.
Pte. Beall, P.G.
Pte. Bedford, S.G.
Pte. Bennett, A.T.
Pte. Beresford, E.A.
Pte. Binyon, J.C.
Pte. Bird, F.J.
Pte. Bland, R.
Pte. Bond, A.L. Killed in action 18/8/16. St. Lukes Wellingborough Northants.
Pte. Bridgman, F. Killed in action 27/9/15. Kettering Northants.
Pte. Broughton, A.E.
Pte. Brown, W.G.
Pte. Bull, A.
Pte. Blades, Wm.
Pte. Boss, G.F.
Pte. Burton, F.W.
Pte. Butcher, W. Killed in action 29/3/17. St. James Northampton.
Pte. Boyson, M. Died of wounds 3/5/16. Creaton Northants.
Pte. Boyson, Wm. Killed in action 26/1/17. Creaton Northants.
Pte. Bettles, A.E. Died of wounds 28/8/16. Colchester Essex.
Pte. Bunning, W.G.
Pte. Carr, E. Killed in action 24/1/17.(Military Medal.) Long Buckby Northants.
Pte. Carter, A.B.
Pte. Carter, A.J. Killed in action 27/9/15. St. Marys

THE MOBBS' OWN

Northampton.
Pte. Carter, E.H. Killed in action 27/9/15. Far Cotton Northampton.
Pte. Carter, E.F.
Pte. Cleaver, E.A.
Pte. Cleaver, R.G. Killed in action 27/9/15. St. Michaels Northampton.
Pte. Coker, E.C.
Pte. Colton, V.M.
Pte. Copson, R. Killed in action 25/3/18. Collingtree, Northants.
Pte. Corbett, R.
Pte. Colton, W.
Pte. Cracknell, F.
Pte. Cunningham, F.
Pte. Cabley, H.
Pte. Cawston, H.
Pte. Carr, G.S.
Pte. Carter, W.
Pte. Clamp, P.V.
Pte. Cox, A.E.
Pte. Deeley, E.W.
Pte. Douglas, A.S.
Pte. Dunkley, L.J. Killed in action 27/9/15. St. Michaels Northampton.
Pte. Driver, H.
Pte. Dodson, I.
Pte. Dunkley, C.F.
Pte. Dunkley, A.J. Killed in action 4/11/18. Rothwell, Northants.
Pte. Dunkley, H.
Pte. Edmunds, J.
Pte. Elfred, J. Died of wounds 27/9/15. Brixworth Northants.
Pte. Facer, P.W.

THE MOBBS' OWN

Pte. Facer, R.G.
Pte. Fancourt, J.E.
Pte. Falkner, P.J.
Pte. Featherstone, H.
Pte. Fisher, A.
Pte. Fitch, C.B. Died of wounds 12/7/16. (Military Medal.) St. Edmunds Northampton.
Pte. Forscutt, S.C. Killed in action 27/9/15. Wellingborough Northants.
Pte. Forskitt, A.
Pte. Faulkner, A.J.
Pte. Gallantry, T.
Pte. Gibbins, T.
Pte. Gilbert, R.E.
Pte. Gilbert, T. Killed in action 25/3/16. Gt. Bowden Leics.
Pte. Gordon, E.
Pte. Granger, E.J.
Pte. Greeves, S.
Pte. Gilbert, J.W.
Pte. Green, E. Killed in action 27/9/15. Cudworth Yorks.
Pte. Garratt, T.A.G. Killed in action 27/9/15. St. Giles Northampton.
Pte. Hammond, W.H.
Pte. Harris, W.
Pte. Head, L.M. Killed in action 27/9/15. Wellingborough Northants.
Pte. Heap, F.A. Killed in action 17/8/16. St. Michaels Northampton.
Pte. Hemmings, H.E.
Pte. Hill, A.
Pte. Hobbs, H.E. Killed in action 27/9/15. Tonbridge Kent.
Pte. Hoddle, F.

Pte. Hollis, G.J.
Pte. House, H.G.
Pte. Hunt, Wm.
Pte. Howes, W.E. Killed in action 27/9/15. Long Buckby Northants.
Pte. Hyde, E. Killed in action 27/9/15. Warboys Hunts.
Pte. Hodgkin, A.R.
Pte. Jeyes, F.
Pte. Johnson, E.T.
Pte. Jones, T.
Pte. Justice, A.E.
Pte. Jennings, W.E.
Pte. Keech, R.B. Killed in action 27/9/15. Brampton Ash Northants.
Pte. Keitch, O.F.
Pte. Kilborn, F.
Pte. King, J.W.
Pte. Kyte, F.G.
Pte. Less, W.A.
Pte. Le Grand, R.
Pte. Letts, J.W.
Pte. Looms, J.
Pte. Luck, A.
Pte. Lambert, H.G.
Pte. Line, A.
Pte. Macalister, J. Killed in action 27/9/15. Gayhurst Bucks.
Pte. Main, H.A.
Pte. Mann, A.E. Killed in action 21/4/16. St. Georges Norwich.
Pte. Manning, J.
Pte. Marriott, Wm.
Pte. Merry, P.S.

THE MOBBS' OWN

Pte. Munroe, A.E. Killed in action 24/2/16. St. Pauls Northampton.
Pte. Murdin, W.H.
Pte. Mynard, R.C.
Pte. Mann, E.V.
Pte. Matthews, J.W. Killed in action 27/9/15. Fairfield Buxton.
Pte. Needham, N.S. Killed in action 27/9/15. St. Crispins Northampton.
Pte. Newman, A. Killed in action 27/9/15. St. Edmunds Northampton.
Pte. North, F. Killed in action 27/9/15. Bourne Lincs.
Pte. North, R.W.
Pte. Nutt, O.M. Killed in action 21/3/18. Newnham Northants.
Pte. Oates, A. Died. 19/3/16. All Saints Northampton.
Pte. Odell, A.J.
Pte. O'Dell, E.R. Killed in action 25/9/15. Bedford.
Pte. Osborne, A.W.
Pte. Osborne, F.J.
Pte. Osborne, R.L.
Pte. Oxley, A.W.
Pte. Owens, W.L.
Pte. Pearson, R.
Pte. Paine, F.E.V. Killed in action 25/9/15. Harpole Northants.
Pte. Peggs, J.W. Died of wounds 29/9/15. Leytonstone Essex.
Pte. Perry, E.L.C.
Pte. Philpot, C.P.
Pte. Parker, V.
Pte. Randall, H.S.
Pte. Rawson, J.G.
Pte. Rice, S.
Pte. Richardson, R.
Pte. Robertson. A.T.

THE MOBBS' OWN

Pte. Robinson, J.R.
Pte. Rowe, H.K. Killed in action 18/8/16. St. Pauls Northampton.
Pte. Rowell, F. Killed in action 27/9/15. St. Lawrence Northampton.
Pte. Rogers, R.C.
Pte. Robinson, G.W.
Pte. Ratcliff, A.S.
Pte. Sedgwick, H. Killed in action 27/9/15. Byfield Northants.
Pte. Shaw, T. Killed in action 27/9/15. Northampton.
Pte. Shepherd, A.R.
Pte. Shephered J.N.K.
Pte. Smith, S.J.
Pte. Simmons, G. Killed in action 3/9/16. Northampton.
Pte. Simons, W.J.
Pte. Simpson, F.
Pte. Smart, W.
Pte. Smith, F. Killed in action 17/8/16. Northampton.
Pte. Smith, J.H.
Pte. Smith, T.J. Killed in action 11/3/16. Littleborough Notts.
Pte. Stevens, G.J.
Pte. Stringer, E.J.
Pte. Stuart, R.E.
Pte. Swann, W. Killed in action 27/9/15. Langley Mill Derbyshire.
Pte. Symonds, S. Died of wounds 17/11/15. Brighton Sussex.
Pte. Strickland, S.
Pte. Swain, F.T.
Pte. Smith, F.E.
Pte. Scillitoe, F.
Pte. Stapleton, C.H.
Pte. Swallow, W.E.

165

THE MOBBS' OWN

Pte. Southwell, H. Killed in action 27/9/15. Kettering Northants.
Pte. Smith, H.
Pte. Tarry, F.
Pte. Tarlton, A. Killed in action 26/1/17. St. Giles Northampton.
Pte. Taylor, H.W. Killed in action 12/4/17. Oundle Northampton.
Pte. Tobin, F.
Pte. Tomlin, P.
Pte. Trott, R.
Pte. Tuckey, W.H.
Pte. Turvey, H.L.
Pte. Twist, T. Killed in action 12/3/16. St. Michaels Northampton.
Pte. Tite, W.H.
Pte. Tite, W.
Pte. Walker, W. Died of wounds 12/10/15. St. James Northampton.
Pte. Ward, H. Killed in action 27/9/15. St. Edmunds Northampton.
Pte. Warwick, J.
Pte. Waters, J.H.
Pte. Watkins, F.E. Killed in action 18/8/16. St. Sepulchres Northampton.
Pte. Westcombe, W.R.
Pte. Wharmby, C.J.
Pte. Whelan, C.J.
Pte. Whilby, S.C.
Pte. Wilford, W.E.
Pte. Wilkinson, A.J.
Pte. Wilkinson, I.
Pte. Willey, J.R.A.
Pte. Williams, A.

Pte. Williamson, H.J.
Pte. Wood, S.
Pte. Wooding, Wm.
Pte. Whitaker, E.T.
Pte. Whitehead, R.W.
Pte. Woodward, R. Died of wounds 5/11/18. Birmingham Warwick.
Pte. Yates, H.

THE MOBBS' OWN